THE PINK WAVE

The Pink Wave

Women Running for Office After Trump

Regina M. Matheson *and* William W. Parsons

NEW YORK UNIVERSITY PRESS

New York

NEW YORK UNIVERSITY PRESS
New York
www.nyupress.org

© 2023 by New York University
All rights reserved

Please contact the Library of Congress for Cataloging-in-Publication data.

ISBN: 9781479826469 (hardback)
ISBN: 9781479826476 (paperback)
ISBN: 9781479826490 (library ebook)
ISBN: 9781479826483 (consumer ebook)

This book is printed on acid-free paper, and its binding materials are chosen for strength and durability. We strive to use environmentally responsible suppliers and materials to the greatest extent possible in publishing our books.

Manufactured in the United States of America

10 9 8 7 6 5 4 3 2 1

Also available as an ebook

CONTENTS

1

She Runs

The Political Landscape for Women Running in the Trump Era

If you can walk away for days, weeks, or years, at a time, it
is not an ambition, it's a wish. Wishes feel good and rarely
come true. Ambition, on the other hand, fuels your days and
refuses to be ignored. It challenges your sense of self and ful-
fills your sense of wonder.
—Stacey Abrams, founder of Fair Fight Action and
former Minority Leader of the Georgia State House
of Representatives

Deciding to run for office is a personal journey. For women, electoral
politics continues to be the road less traveled. While the number of
women running and winning has increased over the past forty years,
representation of women in office remains low compared to their male
counterparts. Historically, only 23 women have run for president from
1872 to 2020 and 11 for vice president from 1884 to 2020. There have
been 417 women who have ever been elected or appointed to serve in
Congress. From 1917 to 1981, there were no more than 20 women serving sequentially in Congress. This number has increased incrementally
since 1983 (the 97th Congress) from 23 women serving to 150 (the 118th
Congress). Women make up a mere 28 percent of the people serving
in Congress. When we observe the number of women serving as state
governors, there have been 49 who have served in thirty-two states and
currently only 12 governors are women. Women have achieved greater
electoral success in state legislatures. Women currently hold 31 percent
of all state legislative seats. While the gap between the number of women

serving in Congress and state legislatures has narrowed, this was not always the case. For instance, in 1991, women made up 18 percent of state legislatures and only 6 percent of the members of Congress. Overall, women have made slight progress in both executive and legislative branches of government.[1]

Despite the incremental increase in women running for office over the past four decades, there have been two noteworthy periods that have spurred women into running for office. The first surge in 1992, dubbed the "Year of the Woman," saw four women elected to the Senate and twenty-four elected to the House of Representatives. Most noteworthy were Barbara Boxer, Diane Feinstein, and Carol Moseley-Braun, who would become fixtures in US politics for decades to come.

The 2016 election results that elevated Donald Trump to the presidency over a disappointed Hillary Clinton shocked, dismayed, and again motivated many women to run for office at all levels of government. Disappointment ensued among women, especially Democrats, at Hillary's loss. Her victory would not only have been historic but would have served as a symbol that the ultimate glass ceiling was shattered. With the election of Donald Trump in 2016, there was a "Second Year of the Woman" during the election cycles of 2018 and 2020, as another pink wave was observed in the number of women elected to Congress, from 105 (114th Congress) to 147 (117th Congress). Additionally, the number of women elected to serve in state legislatures increased from 1,799 in 2016 to 2,295 in 2022.[2] Similar to 1992, the 2018 and 2020 elections cycles produced a number of new women leaders in US politics, including Democrats such as Alexandria Ocasio-Cortez (AOC), Stacey Abrams, and Kamala Harris and Republicans such as Marjorie Taylor Greene and Kim Reynolds.

The surge in candidates in 2018 is analogous to 1992.[3] The prospects for women running and winning congressional seats in 1992 were bolstered by an unusual number of open seats that coincided with a record number of women candidates running in the midst of Anita Hill's allegations of being a victim of sexual harassment by Clarence Thomas. The

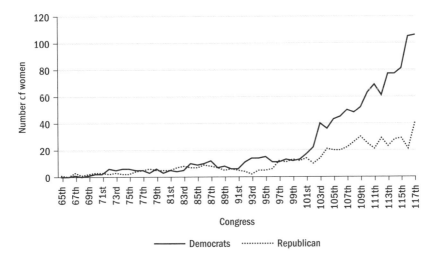

FIGURE 1.1. Women serving in Congress (Center for American Women and Politics)

number of women elected to serve in Congress increased from thirty-two (102nd Congress) to fifty-four (103rd Congress). Figure 1.1 illustrates the number of women who have served in Congress from 1917 to 2022.

In 1992, there was an increase from 18.3 percent to 20.5 percent in women securing state legislative seats nationwide, and in 2018, there was an increase from 25.4 percent to 28.9 percent and another increase in 2020 to 29.3 percent.[4] Perhaps even more salient in 2018 was the election of President Trump in 2016, despite allegations of sexual harassment. The #MeToo movement and a series of women's marches around the nation followed. The 1992 Anita Hill hearings brought sexual harassment to the forefront at a time when it was taboo for female candidates to discuss their own personal experiences with the problem. By 2018, female candidates were more open about their personal experiences, and often those became part of campaigns especially for Democrat candidates.[5] Figure 1.2 highlights the number and percentage of women state legislators from 1980 to 2022.

One distinct parallel between election cycles in 1992 and 2018 and the number of women running for office, especially Democrats, was the

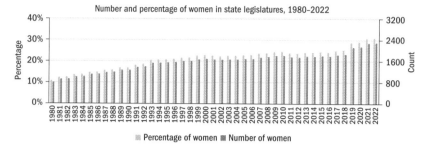

FIGURE 1.2. Number and percentage of women state legislators from 1980 to 2022 (Center for American Women and Politics)

concern over the treatment of women surrounding sexual harassment and sexual misconduct as well as reproductive rights.[6] From the 2016 election of Donald Trump through the 2018 and 2020 election cycles, additional political divisions emerged that were not factors in 1992 electoral politics. Trump's term as president produced three conservative Supreme Court justices—Neil Gorsuch (2017), Brett Kavanaugh (2018), and Amy Coney Barrett (2020)—controversial selections at the time, culminating with the Supreme Court's overturning of *Roe v. Wade* in 2022, with the *Dobbs v. Jackson Women's Health Organization* decision.

Other hotbed issues that framed the post-2016 political landscape revolved around sex/gender, racial inequality, criminal justice reform, gun control, and immigration. Subsequently, polarization on these issues became more pronounced, as illustrated by the intensifying urban-rural divide. While these are common hotbed issues in contemporary politics, they were aggravated by Donald Trump. Unlike in 1992, women who were motivated to run for office after 2016, particularly the state legislature, would encounter a more hostile political environment than had been experienced previously in US politics.[7] In this book, we unveil both positive and negative aspects of Trump-era politics, or the "Trump effect" on how women ran for the state legislature. We explore how this political climate impacted the decision to run and how women ran.

We define the "Trump effect" as the influence of an insurgency candidate, namely, Donald Trump, who elevated voter distrust in government to the point of creating a *chaotic* environment for all candidates from both political parties.[8] Insurgency politics is nothing new to US politics, but rarely has it ever succeeded or had as much impact as Trump's takeover of the Republican Party in 2016.[9]

The Trump effect is not simply about the personal or direct political impact of Donald Trump. The term is applied as a descriptor of US politics since the emergence of Trump on the national political stage circa 2015. While its effects are far-reaching, it has had an observable impact on women running for the state legislature from both political parties. Some of the indicators of the Trump effect in this context include (1) an increased influence of national political trends on state and local elections; (2) a growing "us versus them" approach to politics, an example of which is the urban-rural divide, in which party candidates have fewer opportunities to construct bridges across the political-geographical landscape; and (3) a profound unwillingness to compromise that pushes candidates, of both parties, to seriously consider more extreme policy positions when running for office.

While negative politics is nothing new, we found that the political hostilities during the Trump era were more impactful and far worse than the candidates expected. Women running for the state legislature, by and large, were candidates whose decision to run was less influenced by barriers that have historically discouraged women from running for office. Additionally, women preferred to run campaigns using long-established and accepted strategies and tactics that focused on their individual races. However, voter reactions to President Trump, both positive and negative, were so intense that state legislative candidates had to come to grips with the reality that their campaigns and identities were often being defined by Trump's insurgency politics more than by their individual skills, goals, and agendas.

In this book, we explore the ways in which this chaotic political climate impacted the decision to run and how women ran. We seek to contribute to the discussion on how to expand electoral opportunities for women by analyzing and sharing the experiences of women who ran for the state legislature during two hotly contested major election cycles. This book serves to be both aspirational and inspirational to anyone contemplating running for office in future election cycles.

The 2018 midterm election cycle saw a record number of women running for office at all levels of government. Nowhere was this more evident than in state legislative races throughout the nation. The number of women candidates competing for state legislative seats set a record at 3,395, which was 768 additional candidates than in 2016.[10] When independents, third-party, and nonpartisan candidates are included, the total number of women running (3,418) in 2018 constituted nearly half of state legislative candidates. In the 2020 general election, the record number of women who ran in 2018 was surpassed when 3,446 women ran for the state legislature.[11]

After the 2016 general election, Emily's List reported receiving more than 36,000 inquiries from women interested in learning about how to run for political office. This contrasts with 920 inquiries during the 2016 election cycle.[12] The surge in women running in 2018 was broadly reported to be a function of the national political climate, illustrated by the Trump presidency, the #MeToo movement, women's marches, and hyperpartisanship. Over the past three decades, the number of female candidates running for state legislative seats increased incrementally. Generally the number of women holding state legislative seats has averaged around 22 percent. The 2018 midterm election saw that percentage increase to 28.6 percent of all state legislative seats.[13] In 2020, we saw another incremental increase to 29.3 percent.[14] As figure 1.3 indicates, data from the Center for American Women and Politics (CAWP) and the National Council of State Legislatures (NCSL) document the upward trend in the percentage of women elected to and serving in state legislative seats. The number of women serving in state legislative seats from 2018 to 2020 increased for Democrats, but there was little change for the number of Republican seats during that same time period. Figure 1.4

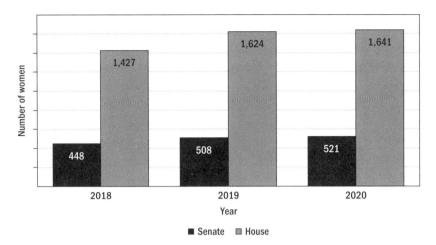

FIGURE 1.3. Women serving in the state legislature by seat in 2018, 2019, and 2020 (Data from Center for American Women and Politics, 2020b, 2020c, 2021b and National Center for State Legislatures, 2018, 2019)

highlights the number of women state legislators by political party for these three years. When including women of color running for and serving in state legislative seats, Democrats increased the number of women of color serving, while Republicans remained about the same from 2018 to 2020. Figure 1.5 depicts the number of women of color serving in state legislatures by political party.

Looking historically over a thirty-year period, the trend remains: more Democrat women candidates have been serving in the state legislature than their Republican counterparts. During this thirty-year period, the number of women serving in state legislatures has increased among Democrats and, at best, has fluctuated among Republicans. Figure 1.6 highlights the number of women in the state legislature by political party from 1990 to 2021. For both parties, the number of women serving in the state legislature may further confirm 2020 as another new "Year of the Woman" for state-level politics, as the number of women serving in state legislatures was at an historic high (759 Republicans, 1,517 Democrats).

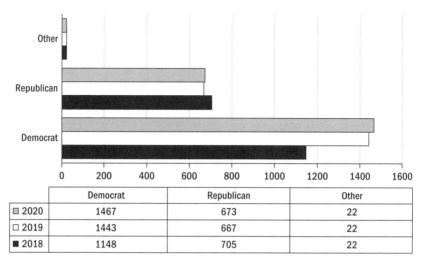

	Democrat	Republican	Other
▦ 2020	1467	673	22
☐ 2019	1443	667	22
■ 2018	1148	705	22

FIGURE 1.4. State seats by party, from 2018 to 2020 (Data from Center for American Women and Politics, 2020b, 2020c, 2021b)

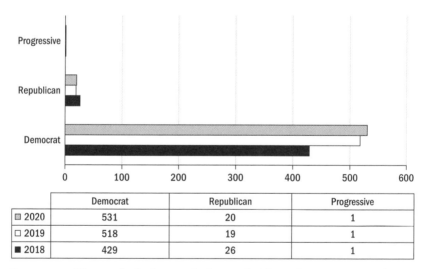

	Democrat	Republican	Progressive
▦ 2020	531	20	1
☐ 2019	518	19	1
■ 2018	429	26	1

FIGURE 1.5. Women of color by party in the state legislature from 2018 to 2020 (Data from Center for American Women and Politics, 2018, 2019b, 2020c)

Will we observe a consistent increase in the number of women running for the state legislature, or do the 2018 and 2020 election cycles suggest something unique about the tensions in the national political climate?[15] And just how differently do women think about the "climate" today compared to past, present, or future elections? One legacy of Trump-era politics is the pressure mounting from the right to return national political agendas to the states, such as reproductive rights. The impact of this movement means that candidates running for the state legislature will find these previously national issues being front and center in future election cycles. With the Supreme Court overturning *Roe v. Wade*, state legislators will now decide the future of reproductive rights. Women may have been motivated to run for the state legislature as a result of Trump-era politics; little did they know at the time that this issue would end up so close to home. None of this would have been fathomable in 1992 or in 2016. The motivation for women to run in upcoming elections may be more intensified because these (women's) social issues have been brought to the forefront and will probably serve as a primary catalyst to enter electoral politics.

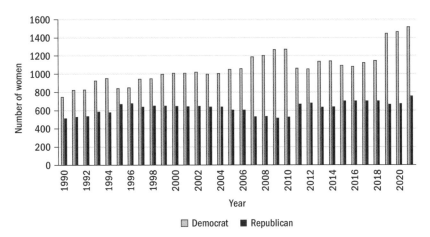

FIGURE 1.6. Women serving in the state legislature by political party from 1990 to 2021 (Data from Center for American Women and Politics, 2021b)

With the surge in female candidates since the 2016 election, we wanted to fully understand the extent to which the decision to run was ostensibly similar or different from past motivating factors. Our mixed-methods approach explored two aspects of the decision of women to run for state legislative seats. First, we examined to what extent the barriers that have historically discouraged women from running were superseded by the national political climate. Additionally, we wanted to understand, after the 2018 midterm election, the factors that respondents attributed to the outcome of their race. In 2020, we wanted to follow up and understand if the factors from 2018 were still an influence for women who ran in 2020.

This book is the culmination of research from national surveys conducted in 2018 and 2020 on women running for state legislative seats in the states that were having elections during the midterm election cycle in 2018 (forty-six states) and in the general election in 2020 (forty-four states). All surveys incorporated closed and open-ended questions. In 2018, we sent two different surveys, one prior to the midterm election and one following the election. The two surveys were sent to the same group of women. Among the survey respondents, the findings indicate that the national political climate in the country was a significant factor in the decision to run for the state legislature and that many of the traditional barriers to women running still existed, but they were superseded by this phenomenon. Postelection respondents were more likely to report that obstacles, such as internal barriers, geographic location, the "Trump effect," and hyperpartisanship, contributed to the outcome of their campaign ($N = 688$ for both 2018 surveys).

A nationwide survey was also conducted in November 2020 with women who appeared on the ballot in the forty-four states holding a state legislative election during the general election cycle. There was only one survey link sent in 2020, and it immediately followed the general election. There were 221 women who responded to the survey. Additionally, 23 women who completed the survey in 2020 participated in an in-depth interview (see the appendix for research methodology, surveys, and in-depth interview questions).

Many interconnected factors influence the decision to run for office. Among them are personal motivation, securing resources, and seeing a strategic opportunity to win.[16] These campaign elements take on a particular meaning for women as they confront historical, societal, and cultural factors that shape their thinking about the ease or difficulty of undertaking the task of navigating the world of politics. For instance, women are less likely to consider themselves qualified to run and more likely to feel that they do not have the time to run, especially if they are already engaged as primary caregivers in addition to working outside the home. Women are also more likely to feel that they are not likely to win.[17] We report the decision-making processes of women running for state legislative seats in 2018 and 2020. We asked what factors they considered and weighed when deciding to run, why they decided to run, how they ran, and how the political climate post-2016 influenced their journey as candidates. Through the surveys and in-depth interviews, several important patterns emerged. We examine these in the following chapters.

The intersection of the national political climate with the decision to run, as seen through the lens of female candidates, is explored in chapter 2. By 2020, the political environment would commonly be referred to as the "Trump effect."[18] This phenomenon was front and center on the minds of the female respondents in our research. This was the case for both Republican and Democrat candidates, often to their dismay. First-time state legislative candidates reported being motivated to run because of the national political climate, often noting the Trump effect as central to their decision. In the 2018 midterm election, the political climate seemed to work to the advantage of Democrat candidates, bringing to the forefront issues that motivated them to run in the first place. By 2020, with Trump on the ballot, Democrat respondents reported a far less friendly political environment. Female Republican respondents raised concerns over the national scene drowning out their personal message targeted for their district.

We put into context the decision to run in 2018 and 2020 with existing research on the barriers historically impacting the entry of women into electoral politics. Barriers that women have confronted when thinking about running for office include their ambition, possessing the required skill set, professional background, caregiving responsibilities, and a lack of party support in the recruitment of candidates. Respondents were cognizant of the barriers confronting women in politics but were able to address them. For some respondents, having a strong support network was critical. Many of the female candidates in our research reported initiating the process to run and would not have run had it not been for what they were witnessing in the national political scene.

As we were poring over the survey results, we noticed three groups of female candidates that appeared to be especially affected by the Trump-era political climate, namely, first-time candidates, rebound candidates, and candidates of color. Thus, chapter 3 provides a more in-depth exploration of female respondents from these three demographic groups. First-time candidates were often motivated to run because of the national political climate. As newcomers to political campaigning, was the experience what they expected? Additionally, we noted the emergence of a number of rebound candidates, women who lost in 2018 and decided to run again in 2020. What motivated them to run again? Did they expect to win or again lose the second time around? Third, as our research progressed across two election cycles, issues related to race had come to the forefront as the 2020 election approached. We wanted to learn more about the emergence of female candidates of color and their efforts to secure a state legislative seat during a political climate that became more and more complex. Finding some answers to these questions could be further revealing as to motivations and commitment of women to run for the state legislature.

In chapter 4, we focus on the experiences of respondents in relation to actually running for the state legislature. For women running as Democrats, the outcome of the 2016 election and the emergence of the Trump effect that followed weighed heavily on their campaigns. As one state legislative candidate noted, "When I would introduce myself to a voter, I would get interrupted and be asked, 'Are you for or against Trump?'"

Hyperpartisanship, or party sorting, heavily impacts today's US politics. Research reveals Americans to be centrists on most issues, but the American people believe that the country is divided.[19] Recent elections, including 2020, show that party sorting was observable in the urban-rural divide, with the suburbs becoming the battleground for swing districts.[20] Our respondents reflected on ways the national political climate impacted their local campaigns. The adage that "all politics is local," made famous by former Speaker of the House Tip O'Neill, seemed more problematic today.[21] Social media has helped to nationalize our political discussions away from local issues.[22]

Additionally, our research reveals that women running as Democrats were concerned about the party's inability to develop easily understandable messaging. Candidates expressed frustration as they sought to present positive messages that sometimes conflicted with their own party's overall messaging and only served to add to the political vitriol. The fear and dread of fundraising is usually front and center here. But other resources are required to fill the bucket, including developing the confidence and competency to campaign and serve as a legislator. We found that while learning about the nuts and bolts of campaigning was important, the primary benefit of professional development was the opportunity to network with other women and build relationships. We end chapter 3 by reporting on whether female candidates perceived that they had any gender-related experiences while running. Given the hostile political climate, respondents viewed most attacks as political and personal, not gender related. The decisions that women make in all aspects of their campaign are important to better understand the role that gender plays in running for office.[23] We contend that a more complete understanding of women in politics requires the inclusion of the political environment in which they are running.

When we began this research project, no one could have predicted that a pandemic would so disrupt our society, let alone during a pivotal election year. While the pandemic was not central to our original thesis, we thought it important to include a separate discussion about the impact of campaigning during COVID-19. We include firsthand accounts of how women candidates navigated the pandemic. Most obvious was a greater reliance on social media platforms such as Twitter, Facebook, and internet advertising. The pandemic reinforced the expanding role of social media in the practice of democracy and political communications.[24] Respondents foresee a markedly changed campaign environment in future election cycles, in which digital platforms become even more central to running for office.

Chapter 5 covers the effects of the urban-rural divide and offers a slightly different take on the impact of the national political climate on state and local politics. The emergence of deep-red and solid-blue political geographic regions in the US suggests that politics, in many respects, is still local. While this divide is real for male and female candidates and for voters, we were interested in asking whether these deep geographic-based divisions helped or hurt the recruitment of women to run for state legislative seats. This is not to imply that women cannot run for office anywhere they choose. We were interested in the extent to which respondents were aware of this divide and whether where they lived mattered in their decision to run. Given the urban-rural divide, opportunities to expand representation of women in state legislatures may continue to grow only incrementally. The areas in which they can run and win are probably more finite due to political-geographic divisions. In this reality, the role of the political party becomes even more important in finding, recruiting, and supporting female candidates in areas where their odds of winning are higher, namely, running female Democrats in blue urban areas and more female Republican candidates in red rural areas.

In chapter 6, we explore what is next for women who decide to run for the state legislature. Among the female respondents, several discussed what needs to happen to encourage more women to run for office. They conveyed valuable lessons from their campaign experiences that future candidates may learn from. Many of the respondents, even if they lost, were not turned off by their campaign experience. Rather, they conveyed a willingness and desire to help other women get involved in politics. Some of the women who lost their races reported that they would run again, while others were content to remain involved in their community and continue to find ways to improve the lives of others. Among those who won, not only were they looking forward to becoming effective legislators, but they also expressed an interest in finding ways to encourage more women to step forward as candidates. Despite the polarization and hotly contested political atmosphere in this country, many of the women who contributed to our research say they will remain committed to public and community service regardless of geographic locale, party affiliation, or competitiveness of their district. Respondents widely reported that they viewed themselves as civically responsible citizens who simply wanted to make a difference. They were not the contentious or stereotypical "war room" candidates often associated with politics and politicians.

A predominant goal of this book is to offer several recommendations for improving the prospects of women achieving equal numbers with men in state legislatures. Many of these have already been suggested in previous research, such as term limits. At the time of this publication, the Nevada State Legislature, which is term limited, was 60 percent female. Nevada appears to have been greatly aided by term limits, requiring long-established incumbent males to step down, thus opening the door for female candidates to emerge.[25]

The value of any recommendation must be calculated against the political climate of the times. We envision our contribution to research on women running for office as different from previous research in that it is a comprehensive examination of the relationship between female candidates and the political landscape in which they operate. The political climate is just as real for women as for men and is often overlooked in the literature. We have written this book to share the experiences of women who ran for the state legislature during a turbulent political climate; however, what we reveal can be applicable to anyone running for office in future election cycles.

2

Deciding to Run

Navigating a Turbulent Political Climate

When day comes, we step out of the shade, aflame and un-
afraid. The new dawn blooms as we free it. For there is always light, if only we're brave enough to see it. If only we're
brave enough to be it.
—Amanda Gorman, former National Youth Poet Laureate

On January 6, 2021, the "Trump effect" was on full display for the world
to observe.[1] Almost four years after the inauguration of the forty-fifth
president of the United States, this effect was consummated when
extremist groups strongly in favor of Trump, holding onto the notion
that the election was stolen from him, invaded the US Capitol Building in Washington, DC, attempting to disrupt the Electoral College vote
count that would favor Joseph R. Biden Jr. Kivisto writes that "for a large
swath of the American population there is an uncomfortable sense that
serious damage has been done to the body politic and to the well-being
of civil society."[2] This statement was written in response to the feeling
that the basic principles of democracy were in question after Donald J.
Trump was elected to office in November 2016. Little did anyone know
just how much the democratic principles that we take for granted would
be called into question over the four years that followed his inauguration. It was on January 6, 2021, that many Americans, even many who
voted for and supported Trump during his four-year tenure as president,
would come to understand just how fragile were the ideals of democracy
in the most powerful democratic government in the world, when the sit-
ting president was accused of inciting violence among his most avid and

committed followers, who marched through the Mall to the US Capitol and in a mob-like fashion stormed the Capitol chambers, where Congress was beginning to count the electoral votes from the November 3, 2020, election.[3]

The "Trump effect," as described by Newman et al., is rooted in language used by Donald Trump that began on the campaign trail and contributes "to a growing body of evidence that Trump's rhetoric shifted social norms and emboldened the prejudiced."[4] There is some evidence of a Trump effect spurring more women to run for office in 2018 and again in 2020. A record number of women ran and won state legislative seats, but they did not win at a rate that reflected the sweeping activism by women following the 2016 election. The legislative seats that women secured in 2018 and 2020, however, surpassed the incremental progress realized over the past forty years, but less than expected given the increased number of women who ran.[5] Among our respondents, Democrats overwhelmingly reported the national political climate as a key factor in deciding to run.

One year after Trump's inauguration, Sword and Zimbardo expanded the definition of the "Trump effect" to include bullying in multiple forms, spanning various demographic groups, as well as misogyny and sexual assault.[6] For many women across the country, the behavior of the president was simply unacceptable. The "Year of the Woman" was regenerated in 2017 and was viewed as a foreshadowing of a "pink wave" of women, particularly Democrats, running for office at all levels including state legislatures.[7] The #MeToo movement and the women's marches across the country that transpired in its wake were associated with an increased interest in women seeking information about running for office as well as increases in the number of women who pursued state legislative seats leading up to the 2018 midterm election.[8] By 2018, female candidates were more open about their personal experiences related to the #Me Too movement, and often those became part of their campaigns, especially for female Democrat candidates.[9] The Trump effect, while a nationally encompassing phenomenon, was seen as particularly impactful to women becoming more politically engaged.[10] What influence did Trump's insurgent politics have on these respondents' considerations about running in spite of the traditional barriers identified in the literature that have historically discouraged women from running for office?

As we seek to better understand the surge in women running for the state legislature in the 2018 and 2020 election cycles, both historical barriers to running and current political conditions were factored into the analysis. Barriers to women running have existed and have been covered in the literature over the past forty years. Some of the traditional barriers that women consider when deciding to run for state legislative office include political ambition, family and caregiving responsibilities, engaging in a profession that would traditionally lead to a career in politics, and having an appropriate skill set to run for office and serve.[11] The important and timely question we sought to answer was whether the national political climate superseded the barriers that have traditionally weighed on the minds of women when they contemplated running for the state legislature.

Historically, for women who have run for public office and served, many begin with local-level politics because of these traditional barriers, even when their aspirations may be to serve at the state level or other higher-level office.[12] For many of our respondents, particularly those running for the first time, the tipping point for deciding to run was the national political climate that surfaced after the 2016 election. We also considered traditional barriers to women running for the state legislature, such as political ambition, professional background and skill set, and family caregiving responsibilities. Understanding how the women in our research experienced these interlocking factors provides a context for better understanding where things stand for the prospects of more women running and winning in ever-changing political environments. Our research reveals that the national political climate after the election of Donald J. Trump in 2016, while complex, weighed heavily on the decision to run for these respondents, despite barriers that have been reported to dissuade women from running.

Political Ambition

Political scientists employ an ambition framework to explain the decision to run for office.[13] This model assumes that personal ambition is a driving force behind stepping up to enter the electoral arena. Commonly held assumptions about women are that they lack the same political ambition as men. In addressing this question, Fulton et al. and Clark et al. found that women had more ambition to run for higher office when they could see a likelihood of winning. Women are also more likely to enter the fray when they calculate that political and institutional factors are in their favor.[14] Additionally, it has been argued that when women decide to run for office, they should be better candidates than their male counterparts.[15]

Utilizing survey data collected by the CAWP, Carroll and Sanbonmatsu found that the ambition framework does not provide a complete picture of how women come to decide to run for office.[16] Historically, women have been more likely to run for the state legislature when approached by someone in their personal or political network. In our research, we found many examples of women running after someone had approached them, but when taking into consideration the national political climate after the 2016 presidential election, there were many examples of women running as a result of what they perceived to be occurring in the nation.

There were a number of respondents who became actively involved in political efforts following the election of Trump in 2016. One respondent, despite commenting that she and her friends should consider a bid for office, still needed to be recruited to run. She wrote,

> I was recruited. I had said something off the cuff with some friends a couple of months after Trump was elected about how "we should all run for office!" One of my friends who was there was on the local committee to recruit candidates, so, later that year she called me and said, "Remember when you said you'd run? Well, how about now?" I had not thought

seriously about it at all. But when she asked, my almost immediate response was "yes." (2020, Democrat, North Carolina)

Another respondent, recruited by the Democratic Party, indicated that her desire to run was influenced by the national political climate:

I was recruited. My Democratic Party chair had asked me several times to run for an office, and given the current climate, I agreed. (2018, Democrat, Connecticut)

Another respondent whose activism was sparked following the 2016 election discussed her experience with being recruited:

I was recruited. I cofounded an Indivisible group after the 2016 election, and while we started it because of concerns about protecting health care, education, voting rights, immigration, and other issues at the national level, we quickly realized that our state had many issues that needed immediate attention. After we grew to over one thousand members within two years and helped influence the 2018 election, the chair of my legislative district approached me about running for the statehouse. I never imagined I'd run for office and actually told her no six times before finally saying yes. I decided it was a unique opportunity to be part of making a big difference for a lot of people, especially for underserved children and families in our state. (2020, Democrat, Arizona)

For those respondents who cited their ambition to run for office, many still had self-doubt but ran once someone suggested that they consider running. It is interesting that many women in 2020 still needed some reassurance that they were qualified to run and should consider it. One respondent, when asked the question whether she initiated running or whether she was approached, shared this response:

I always believed I would run, but as an IT professional, I was unsure of the path. I did as I always do: I put my energy to good use, and one fateful night while at a fundraiser for a local candidate, a woman began grilling me after I asked her what a good candidate would look like in my district that had traditionally been red. She then asked me point blank, "You are clearly intelligent, articulate, passionate about issues and your community. Why don't you run?" Before I could respond, she called over the then-minority leader in the House and suggested we have coffee. I drove home wondering what had just happened. But the more I thought, the more I realized it felt right, and the elation and the nervousness rose. We did meet for coffee and a few questions, but what neither the woman nor the leader knew was the seed had long been planted in me. I used to deliberately route my car past the Capitol whenever in the area to marvel at it, and I recall vividly once standing on the lawn in front of the Capitol with certainty in my heart that one day I would work there. I belonged there years before that fateful night. I believed it was my destiny to serve. I believed I could win. I knew it would be hard in what most believed to be a reliably red district. My first cycle, I had no help or targeting. No one believed I could win, but I told them I knew it was possible and proved it two years later. I am now in my second term. I hope my community will continue to give me the opportunity to serve. Few people can live their purpose. I believe this is mine—to serve my community and create positive change. (2020, Democrat, Minnesota)

Interestingly, this respondent had to be asked rather than self-initiating a run for office, despite the fact that she had a longtime desire to serve in the state legislature.

Political parties and community organizations are important gatekeepers and recruiters of candidates. It matters whether recruitment of women is framed as a supply or demand problem. If women see the opportunities available as a function of an inadequate supply—not enough qualified candidates—then the chances of feeling qualified to run decrease.

Demand increases when gatekeepers actively recruit more women candidates.[17] Both of these factors are evident in research that points out that women are more likely to be recruited in areas where the political parties have trouble finding candidates.[18] If we consider initiating the process as a measurement of ambition, we find that men report, by a two to one margin, that running is entirely their own idea when compared to women. In contrast, almost twice as many women than men report being recruited to run.[19] Political party "gatekeepers" are increasing their efforts to close the gender gap. Nevertheless, some biases in where to look for candidates is apparent. For women who rely more on being recruited to run rather than initiating the process to run themselves, they are also more likely to question their skill set and how their background would fit with the elected position, especially at the state level.[20]

Alleviating anxiety and gaining confidence that one has adequate skills and experiences goes beyond simply deciding to run. The anxiety about whether one indeed should be running for office was reinforced by a newly elected legislator who drove to the Capitol and observed the legislature in session to become more comfortable with running for a seat. She was elected to the seat but felt compelled to familiarize herself with the lay of the land despite a long career in public service.

If women continue to question their experience and how it relates to positions that they could occupy, it will continue to discourage them from pursuing those positions. One respondent implied that there are differences when it comes to men and women when approached about running for office:

> Women wait to be asked. I didn't. I just ran, which is much more of a male type of attitude. Women have to be persuaded. When you're going to run for office, you've got to be all in. How is it that you teach women to not have to be asked or to wait and be asked and, instead, have them say they want to learn more about running? I think that's really important. (2020, Democrat, Indiana)

Another respondent discussed the reason that she ran and how women have to consider more when running than a man may have to:

> If I had gotten elected, I would have such a huge learning curve. I am almost glad I didn't win. I didn't run to just be elected. I thought about what benefit I could bring to the job. I can't unknow what I know so far, so something's got to give. Whether it is my name on the ballot or not, I would be happy to help anyone run. The biggest joke at one of the women's campaign schools was that women have to think about it. I have four children and needed a lot of help to manage to do this campaign. It was eighteen hours a day, seven days a week, for six months straight. They joke that men need a flag pen, and that's it. They sign their name and run for office. (2020, Republican, tri-state area, East Coast)

Although the desire to run is a significant and necessary motivator for many respondents, some of them questioned whether their passion, experiences, and skill sets were adequate to be considered a serious and viable candidate. The intersection of political ambition and the skills one can bring to electoral politics is something that women weigh as they contemplate running. There were plenty of respondents who decided to run in 2018 and/or in 2020 who did so only after evaluating themselves against their potential opponents. Perhaps this was related to the political climate and women evaluating what they could bring to the table as superlative to others. One of these respondents, when asked what impacted her decision to run, stated,

> [I was] angry at my state government's dysfunction and inability to move our state forward. The seat was open because the incumbent termed out, and it was being sought after by a person I deemed completely unable to adequately do what I believed was in the best interest of the state. I was convinced that there were not others who had stepped up to run for the open seat, and there was concern—I frankly wanted someone else

to run, and I would support them. But that wasn't happening, and I felt a sense of responsibility to put my money where my mouth was. (2020, Democrat, Oklahoma)

Professional Background and Skill Set

Fox and Lawless found evidence that women are as highly qualified as men yet are less likely to be recruited by the major political parties.[21] When comparing men and women as potential recruits who are coming from the same professional spheres (business, law, political activism, education), women were less likely to be approached to run than men.

The traditional model of recruitment into electoral politics has a bias toward legal and business professional backgrounds and those who are already involved in local politics or in the political party.[22] Data collected about professional experience in our 2020 survey are consistent with what has been reported in the literature over the past forty years: that individuals with backgrounds in legal, education, and business professions make up a large majority of individuals seeking office.[23] Of the respondents in our 2020 survey, 39 percent reported having a background in one of these three professions.

Female candidates are more likely than men to come from health care and education careers and are less likely to possess advanced degrees.[24] Of the 221 respondents to our 2020 survey, 129 reported having earned a graduate degree, and 66 reported having earned at least a bachelor's degree (total 88 percent). Likewise, data from the 2018 survey revealed a similar pattern with regard to educational attainment: 87 percent of the respondents reported having earned a bachelor's degree or higher.

Fox and Lawless found evidence that backgrounds in health care have emerged as a pathway into politics.[25] Of the 220 respondents reporting about their profession in our 2020 survey, 18 respondents indicated a background in health care. One respondent from the 2018 survey confirmed the importance of the health-care perspective. When asked what else she considered prior to running, she responded,

> The need for medical professionals to take part in decisions made around health-care policy, the desire to improve the lives of my patients. (2018, Democrat, Colorado)

Another respondent was confident that her background in local government service was sufficient to run for the state legislature:

> The only real factor is that I understand my district and community and feel, with my experience in local school and municipal governance, I am uniquely qualified to understand the issues and advocate for my constituents. (2018, Democrat, Maine)

In this example, experience in public service helped this respondent frame that she was qualified to run. Developing confidence from prior community involvement also increases political ambition in women.[26] Another respondent concurred. When asked the question "What other factors did you consider when running for the state legislature?" she replied,

> I have worked on legislation at the state level and across the country for over a decade and had a desire to serve my community. (2018, Democrat, Massachusetts)

It is not uncommon for women to undervalue their skill set and have lower self-confidence than their male counterparts when it comes to evaluating their professional abilities, particularly when it comes to politics.[27] Many of the respondents in our study reported being doubtful about having the appropriate background and skill set to run for and serve in the state legislature and about whether they would be perceived as a "qualified candidate." One respondent, when asked why she would question her skill set when she had served in two local public office seats, had family experiences that would be informative to legislation, and also held an associate's degree, stated,

> Quite honestly, I never thought that this would be open to me. . . . I never would have started at this level had I not already held other offices. (2020, Republican, Ohio)

She discussed, however, being very encouraging to others who would be serving in the upcoming state legislature and who had not held elected office and lacked that experience, but she continued to question her own qualifications for the position she was elected to.

How candidates feel about their own qualifications or skill set can also influence their sense of readiness or political ambition. Women are far more confident about running for office today than nearly forty years ago and see prior political experience as less important.[28] Women, in general, report that they are held to higher standards when compared to their male counterparts and feel they have to work harder and be more credentialed to get the same respect or level of recognition as, perhaps, a male counterpart would. It was Amy Klobuchar who called our attention to this issue. When standing on the stage at the Democratic Party primary debate on November 20, 2019, she made the comment, "Of the women on the stage, do I think that we would be standing on that stage if we had the same experience he had [referring to Pete Buttigieg]? No, I don't. Maybe we're held to a different standard."[29]

Individuals are socialized to understand who should or can be in specific social positions in society, resulting in an unconscious or implicit bias about individuals on the basis of their sex/gender, race/ethnicity, socioeconomic status, age, and so on. There are ample research and examples of the impact of unconscious/implicit bias related to sex/gender that suggest that a significant portion of the population believes that certain careers are best suited for men or for women and that the number of men and women we see in certain occupations or professional positions continues to reflect such biases.[30] One respondent shared the following comment:

> You have to dance backwards in heels. It is the same as my career as a trial attorney. Men do not take me seriously, and they are condescending. I have to prove at every point that I am better than them to be perceived as acceptable. (2018, Democrat, North Carolina)

The depth and breadth of unconscious sex/gender bias is pervasive, and such gendered perceptions reinforce stereotypes that typically get ingrained at a very young age. Because a number of biases are disproportionately focused on sex/gender, the consequences for females have an impact that begins in early childhood and shape what women pursue and how they approach that pursuit throughout adolescence and adulthood.[31] One way that girls get socialized into gender roles is through insinuations that they are too loud or that they are being bossy. This gets internalized, as females are socialized to mute their voice and be quiet and not be assertive. How do women navigate these gendered messages and still pursue occupations, professions, and promotions that society perceives as masculine and that have historically been more open to their male counterparts, particularly in politics?[32] One respondent spoke specifically about the impact of gender bias in electoral politics:

> This might sound weird, but I think being a woman can hurt and help you. In the Democratic Party, women in leadership is more common. In rural Republican states, it's still fairly patriarchal. There are unconscious biases related to competency/leadership in women. Also, to advance in a man's world, you have to learn how to drink whisky, fish, and talk sports. Luckily, I had a career before that prepared me. I had to drink a lot of whisky and talk a lot of hunting to get to that point. Women have to learn about things we're not exposed to, or even like, in order to advance—even in politics. (2020, Republican)

It has been reported in both the mainstream media and academic literature that an unconscious or implicit bias exists in society, especially in the minds of voters, and has consequences for individuals contemplating running for office, especially women and minorities.[33] Perceptions of a candidate's competence gets evaluated based on traditional gender roles that perpetuate implicit gender bias. Additionally, perceptions of traditional gender roles are alive and well in the minds of voters as they consider who is the more qualified and competent candidate to serve.[34]

Qualities such as competitiveness, decisiveness, and strength are the very qualities we expect to see in someone running for office, but we expect that, once elected, those serving in a political office will adopt qualities historically associated with feminine gender ideologies, such as cooperation and collaboration.[35] Female candidates are struck by the reality that when running for office, they may need to adhere to more masculine gender ideologies such as being competitive and decisive but also need to balance those with traditional feminine gender ideologies, to which females are expected to adhere, such as being cooperative, nurturing, and passive. Not only does the gender-ideology balancing act become front and center when women evaluate their skill set and contemplate running for office, but it plays out when they are in the midst of campaigning and running. One respondent implied that she had engaged in self-evaluation as it relates to running:

> I was a good fit politically for the district, I thought I could win, and I wanted to serve. (2020, Republican, Florida)

Another respondent spoke to the gender-ideology characteristics that she thought as a woman candidate would be beneficial if she were elected:

> One advantage I think I have as a woman is my innate ability to build relationships and to listen. Regardless of political affiliation, I am able to connect with voters. This will be helpful if I win. We need more cooperation and collaboration in the House. (2018, Democrat)

The respondents in our research commented about contemplating what they might bring to the table as well as engaging in a great deal of research to reassure themselves that they could do the job. One respondent confirmed that her qualifications were weighing on her decision to run. When asked, "What other factors did you consider when running for the state legislature?" she responded, "my own qualifications."

Several respondents mentioned that when they compared themselves to their male opponents, the men seemed more confident in their skill sets and professional background and deemed them as adequate regardless of their experience or how their background may contribute to running for or holding office. One respondent confirmed that she was evaluating her experience in relationship to running. When asked the question, "What other factors did you consider when running for the state legislature?" she responded,

> Do I have the skill set to address critical issues facing our state. (2018, Democrat, Washington)

Another respondent replied,

> Whether I could bring something to the job. (2018, Democrat)

Another commented on the importance of the intersection of these barriers to running and the impact running may have on one's family:

> Balancing the elected role with a professional occupation. Ability to manage your household while serving in office. Being a primary caregiver to family members. (2020, Republican)

It is not uncommon for women to professionally evaluate themselves more critically and less confidently than their male counterparts do. Plenty of recent literature exists about the "confidence gap" between men and women, the impact it has on success, and the deep roots, in general, to gender socialization but, more specifically, how it inter-sects with political socialization.[36] When it comes to male-dominated or historically masculine professions, such as elected office or politics, adopting a more masculine persona may positively impact the success of female political candidates who want to break into politics.[37] How-ever, as female candidates, women also have to delicately balance mas-culine traits that society deems as imperative to running and holding office with more feminine traits that may contribute to being a success-ful politician.

Family and Caregiving Responsibilities

An additional barrier to women considering running for office is fam-ily and caregiving considerations. The Pew Research Center reports that mothers today spend about twice as much time on child care as fathers do.[38] While the amount of time spent on child care has increased for both mothers and fathers since the mid-1980s, caregiving respon-sibilities continue to fall predominantly on mothers in the household, regardless of whether they are working. In 2011, about 71 percent of men and 62 percent of women aged sixteen to sixty-four were employed. Women were spending less time on housework in 2011 (15 hours per week) than they were in 1965 (28 hours per week), while men have increased the number of hours engaged in housework for the same time period, increasing from 4 hours per week in 1965 to 9 hours per week in 2011 (figure 2.1).

From 1965 to 2011, the time that married mothers focused on child care increased from 10.6 to 14.3 hours per week, while the time married fathers devoted to child care increased from 2.6 to 7.2 hours per week. When single parents are included in this analysis, both single mothers and single fathers increased the time they spent with their children. From 1986 to 2011, single mothers increased the time they spent with their children from 5.8 hours per week to 11.3 hours per week, and the time that single fathers spent with their children increased from less

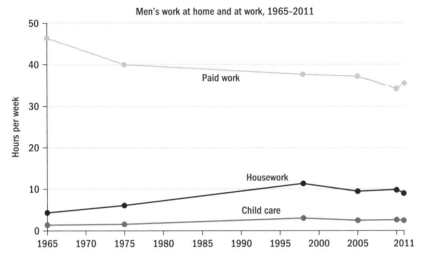

FIGURE 2.1. Comparing the time that mothers and fathers spend caring for children per week from 1965 to 2011 (Pew Research Center, 2013)

than 1 hour per week to about 8 hours per week. In general, American mothers still spend about twice as much time with their children as fathers do. Caregiving responsibilities in the US still fall primarily on women, regardless of whether they are married or single. For women who are contemplating a career or a run in electoral politics, one of the primary factors to consider is the impact of doing so on their family and the ability to balance work and professional obligations with managing a household and caregiving.

Candidates who are married need a strong and supportive commitment from their partner or spouse to consider running for office in general but especially when they have children or caregiving responsibilities, along with a career. One respondent discussed the importance of her spouse and his support:

My husband was 100 percent supportive and willing to do whatever needed to be done with the kids and household. If I didn't have a spouse who pulled his weight, I couldn't have done it. (2020)

Another respondent, when asked what other factors she considered in her decision to run, commented,

> It mattered to me whether my wife would welcome this addition to our lives together. She does. (2018)

Single mothers who consider a bid for office also need strong support from family and friends when they have caregiving responsibilities and may have to decide on a career in politics or a professional occupation, because they may have more difficulty juggling both. A single mother who had recently adopted a child discussed how this impacted her decision to run:

> Balancing an elected role with an occupation—I am a professor at a state university, so I intentionally separated the two. During the campaign, I became a first-time, single parent to a child through adoption, which was a game changer for my life, [both] professional and personal. (2018)

Another single mother stated,

> Being a primary caregiver most impacted my decision to run. I am a single mother, and I have worked multiple jobs to make sure my kids had a roof over their heads, clothes on their backs, and food on the table. There wasn't much left after that. I don't want this to be the same way either of my children or someday grandchildren have to struggle with. (2020)

Maintaining caregiving responsibilities for children younger than eighteen poses specific challenges to those who are contemplating running for office—a barrier that continues to be reported in the literature even forty years after it was identified as a major obstacle for women who may want to enter electoral politics.[39] One candidate who was married with small children shared her concerns about running for office. When asked what other factors she considered as she decided to run for office, she stated,

How it would impact my family. I have a three-and one-year-old at home. (2018)

Many married respondents with children younger than age eighteen, when asked what other factors influenced their decision to run, shared similar comments:

Impact on my family, ability to hold another job. (2018)

Impact on personal life and career. (2018)

My ability to continue working at my job when legislature not in session. (2018)

Support of friends and family, but mostly whether or not I could run for office while also working, being a mother to two small children and serving on city council. (2018)

The ability to have a balance between my children and husband, while also serving my state and district. (2020)

There were 162 of 679 (24 percent) respondents from our 2018 surveys who reported having children younger than eighteen. In 2020, 80 of 220 (36 percent) respondents reported having children younger than eighteen. For many women candidates, they run for office when they no longer have caregiving responsibilities at home for their children and/ or are retired from their profession. Many respondents made comments that were consistent with this. One respondent stated,

> I have the time [to run] now that children are grown to devote to politi-
> cal service. Family obligations will not impede my ability to serve. (2018,
> married)

One respondent commented that she retired in order to run for office, and even though she had children who were no longer living in the home, she was still concerned about how a run for office would impact her family:

> [I considered the] impact on my family, the time commitment. I retired
> from a thirty-plus-year career to run for office. (2018, married)

Most women legislators first run for office around age fifty, after caregiving responsibilities have diminished, even though securing the support from of a partner remains an important factor in the decision.[40] This is consistent with respondents in our study. One respondent spoke to this issue when she commented,

> I ran because progressive voters needed a choice/voice against a conser-
> vative incumbent, and recent elections have shown that the number of
> progressive voters in this community is growing. I have been organizing
> in this community for several years, and we needed someone to run to
> continue our progress. The fact that my children are grown and that my
> part-time job gives me more freedom than some other folks enabled me
> to run when others couldn't. (2020, Democrat)

The average age of respondents in our research in 2018 and in 2020 was around fifty-two (see table 3.1 in chapter 3). According to Johnson and Stanwick, women wait to run for office until they have fewer caregiving responsibilities for their own children.[41] For women candidates who wait to run until they are middle-aged or retired or whose children are grown, they may encounter caregiving responsibilities related to aging parents or relatives. According to the National Alliance for Caregiving,

61 percent of all adult family caregivers are women, and the average age of a caregiver is fifty-one. The number of caregivers has increased to 41.8 million in 2020, from 34.2 million in 2015.[42]

Caregiving responsibilities for women political candidates may not cease once their children become adults. They may be immediately confronted with caregiving to aged parents or other aged relatives. As society continues to gray, this may be an additional barrier to women running for office. At the same time, there may be a greater need to have women engaged in electoral politics who have experienced these life circumstances, as policy and legislation is shaped to assist family caregivers. For our 2018 and 2020 surveys, 42 percent of respondents reported not having caregiving responsibilities for children or other relatives. In 2020, we asked respondents how they considered being a primary caregiver impacted their decision to run. For those respondents who were providing care to aging relatives whether inside or outside their home (n = 46/221), 54 percent indicated that this was moderately or extremely important to their decision to run.

As a society, we miss out on a large swath of perspectives by discounting the contributions that female caregivers can make to organizations.[43] In politics, the dearth of women caregivers in the legislature raised the following alarm for one respondent:

> There are very few young mothers represented in the legislature. This is a travesty because our stage of life has a lot to offer in terms of the impacts of legislation on our daily lives. We are whose rights are being legislated. We should have a voice. (2018, Republican)

Another respondent, when asked, "What other factors did you consider when running for the state legislature?" replied,

> The impact on my family and if I was appropriate representation for the district. (2018, independent)

In addition to questioning whether she would be a good representative for her district, she was also aware that running for office would have an impact on her family. Another respondent, even though she was not a primary caregiver, knew that running would impact the time she could spend with her mother:

> Although I'm not a primary caregiver, my mother, who is now ninety-one and lives over eighty miles from me, loves company and needs to go to doctor appointments, etc. I love to spend time with her and knew running would cut into that time. When I first ran, I didn't really know how much. Being able to run my household from afar was also a concern. I can leave my house with no problem but have guilt pangs over leaving my dog for days at a time. Taking him with me just doesn't work because of housing and crazy hours. (2020, Democrat)

In two-career households, female would-be candidates are still likely to bear the responsibility for the "second shift" when it comes to managing the household and caregiving.[44] Work-life circumstances, such as caregiving responsibilities, typically impact women more than men.[45] One respondent commented about all the factors related to family and career that she had to consider prior to running:

> For dual-income families, it will be the cost of decreased income. In some cases, it might be falling behind in your career, sort of like when women leave the workforce to have children. In families with children, it will be the reality that women are still the primary caregivers in families. Even in my home, where I have a twenty-four-year-old who lives miles away, I'm still responsible for everything related to our finances, household, and health care. My husband doesn't even know the password to our bank accounts. If the dishwasher breaks, I coordinate and pay the repairman. If our dogs need to go to the vet, I do that too. My husband doesn't even make his own doctor appointments. I set out his prescription meds every day and pack his lunch. Oh yeah, then there's my career. (2020, Republican, Montana, won)

Nevertheless, Fox and Lawless conclude that family considerations are not a primary factor in determining political ambition among women.[46] They recognize that parental status and division of labor in the home affect whether women will run, but these types of work-life balance factors do not in and of themselves explain women's levels of political ambition when compared to men. For women, political ambition may be high, but when caregiving responsibilities and household management get factored into the equation of running, their prospects of running may diminish. Our research reveals that many respondents did consider how the decision to run and running for office would affect their family. One respondent stated,

> Work/Life/Campaign Balance—I think women want to do it all, and realistically something has got to give. I ended up going to 80 percent time for my job. I missed many critical moments with my infant/toddler, my seven-year-old was constantly complaining about how much time I spent campaigning, and my husband had to pick up all the slack— cooking, cleaning, child care, transportation, etc. Women still carry so much of the emotional work in a household. It's very difficult to manage something as intense as a campaign + a job + a household, unless you are independently wealthy and can hire housekeepers and nannies. (2020, Democrat, won)

Another respondent replied,

> Being able to manage my household, maintain my caregiving roles in my family, and continue with my work outside of session, while giving my elected position my all as well. It can be tough to balance everything. (2020, Democrat, caregiver to children and aging relatives)

For some families, the option to run was more appealing because there were additional family members residing in the home who could share household responsibilities. One respondent spoke to this and stated,

I probably would not have run if my thirty-five-year-old daughter didn't live with us with her children. She would be able to help my husband keep the household running if I couldn't be home. The drive to Denver and the fact that Denver has become a dangerous place to be also had to be taken into consideration. (2020, Republican)

One of the benefits that many women who ran considered, or perhaps justified their running and being away from their children, was to be a role model to family members and to ensure representation among mothers in the state legislature. One respondent stated,

The competitiveness of the seat, the fact that no women had ever held it and there are no mothers of young children in our legislature, and being an example to my children about trying to make the community a better place. (2020, Democrat, Tennessee)

Another respondent replied,

Because poor, single moms and people from the field of social work deserve a voice in the legislature too. (2020, Democrat)

Another respondent stated,

I am a mother. I am modeling being the change I want to see. (2020, Democrat)

Respondents consistently mentioned that a shorter distance to the state capital and the importance of being home every night were positive influences for them to run. This geographical constraint has been recognized as a barrier that has an influence on whether women even consider running. The farther away a candidate is from the capital, especially those with caregiving responsibilities, the less likely they are to run for office.[47] In our 2018 survey, respondents reported an average distance of 102 miles to the capital (median = 63; range = 2–848). In 2020, respondents reported an average distance of 101 miles to the capital (median = 61.6; range = 2–925). One respondent discussed how proximity to the state capital would impact her family:

> Ability to manage my family and child responsibilities was important, as well as living close enough to the capital so I didn't have to stay overnight and be away from my family for extended periods of time. (2020)

Another respondent replied,

> I'm still figuring out how to set boundaries around work. My family is close to the capital, and we will make an effort to have family dinners. It is also very important to my partner that he is included in helping manage campaign tasks. (2018)

Another respondent had a solution to this problem so that she did not have to decide between the legislature and her family:

> My family will be moving with me to the state capital so that I can spend more time with my son during the legislative session. (Democrat, won)

Another respondent, when discussing how she was going to manage the balance of motherhood with being a state legislator, stated,

> I'm sure it will be a challenge. I have three- and six-year-old boys, and I've been home with them for the past six years. But like millions of American families, we'll figure it out. I'm lucky that Rhode Island is so small and I can get to the statehouse in twenty-five minutes! (Democrat, won)

At just about every conference that focuses on women, there is typically a session or discussion on work-life balance. Women who decide to run for a state legislative office do so recognizing that the decision requires finding a way to balance family with politics. Understanding that women continue to be primary caregivers to children as well as aging family members and are primarily responsible for managing the household, we thought it was important to ask respondents specifically how they planned to manage the work-life balance if they were elected to serve. We only asked the question in 2018. The responses were interesting yet not surprising. Three respondents asked, "Does this question get asked of men or male legislators?" and to them, we would respond that if it does not get asked, maybe it should.

Many respondents commented that they had already sorted out how to approach this balance prior to running, whether it was with a job and having to negotiate work hours, a leave of absence, quitting work, or retiring. One respondent commented,

> I will balance my work as a full time HS [high school] teacher with my work as a legislator, but I doubt I'll have much of a "personal" life. Thank goodness my husband is very self-sufficient and supportive. (Democrat, won)

One respondent who had negotiated how to balance work with the legislature stated,

> I am able to reduce my work load without a significant impact on my salary. At least that's what I am hoping. We haven't spoken formally yet. Plus, I am on sabbatical in the spring. The legislature is part-time, so the spring semester is the only term affected. (Democrat, won)

One respondent in 2020 noted the importance of her employer's flexibility to her ability to run:

> I ran in 2016 for the first time, and the fact that I am privileged enough to be able to leave a job for a year in order to run and forgo the salary, but also know the job would still be there if I was not successful. (2020, Democrat)

Others commented about the importance of planning and having a set schedule as well as having a really supportive partner or hiring a housekeeper or a nanny. One respondent stated how important it was to her to find this balance and why:

Life balance is extremely important, and finding it is an ongoing challenge. Things are evolving as my children are all in college now, and I am finding that part easier. I had a health event this year, though, so taking care of my health and well-being is a priority. (Democrat, won)

Another respondent reiterated the importance of a supportive spouse:

It's all a matter of planning and staying organized. I will schedule trips and days off to see my adult children and will make sure I make time for my husband. Having a supportive husband, which I have, is key. (Democrat, won)

Another respondent replied,

It's hard with young kids. I avoid a lot of receptions and work dinners so I can get home to my kids. Also, we have a nanny who lives with us. (Democrat)

Two respondents in 2020 mentioned the work-life balance even though we did not ask specifically about the topic. One of those respondents stated,

Being able to manage my household, maintain my caregiving roles in my family, and continue with my work outside of session, while giving my elected position my all as well. It can be tough to balance everything. (2020, married, children younger than eighteen)

Another respondent discussed the role of her partner in the balance of work and family:

The support of my partner was very important, being able to afford to take a pay cut from my regular job, and being able to balance parenting with the schedule of the legislature. (2020, married, children younger than eighteen)

Many other respondents indicated that they had no idea how they were going to find a work-life balance while serving.

A plethora of literature over the past forty years indicates that family caregiving responsibilities pose a barrier for women considering running for political office beyond the local community. To date, this is a consideration that weighs heavily on women regardless of their ambition. When taking into consideration one's political ambition coupled with a positive assessment of the skill set one has to offer as a state legislative candidate, women contemplating running for office who were also caregivers in 2018 and in 2020 realized that it was important for their perspectives to be represented in the legislature. For many, to get to that point was not an easy decision.

Conclusion

The barriers to women running for office or the factors that women must consider or should consider prior to running may not be unique for women, but how women consider the traditional barriers to running and their experiences when contemplating how these traditional barriers will impact their campaign may very well differ from the considerations of their male counterparts.[48] These unique experiences of women deciding to run for state legislative office during a volatile political climate since 2016 are what we intended to capture in this chapter.

Of the respondents to our surveys, many described how the political climate impacted their political ambition regardless of whether they had a typical path into electoral politics, the skill set, or the background to run for a state legislative seat. We believe that the traditional barriers perceived by women when it comes to influencing their decision to run will probably always exist and persist regardless of the political climate in which they are running. However, volatile political climates may spark political ambition in women candidates who do not feel the need to be recruited or who dismiss the typical skills and background as less important to a successful campaign and what they can bring to the legislative seat.[49] This is what we observed in the data. Women in our study conveyed how the Trump effect and the volatile political environment after 2016 influenced their decision to run when they may not have considered it otherwise.

We have scratched the surface of answering the question that may still remain: Did the chaotic political climate and Trump's insurgency politics supersede the barriers that have historically impacted women's decisions to run for office? In sum, the response to this question is yes. Overwhelmingly, the respondents revealed that the political climate was a factor in their decision to run for the state legislature. The subsequent chapters discuss more in-depth what impact the Trump effect had on specific groups of women candidates after 2016 and how these women ran during these two election cycles. One respondent, after deciding to run, shared a piece of advice that will resonate with any candidate who has ever decided to enter electoral politics:

> This is hard. So very, very incredibly hard. And it's important to go into this with no expectations, a thick skin, and to have the support of friends and family. I may have a lot of support, but it's still an incredibly lonely journey. (2018, Democrat, running for the first time)

3

Making History

First-Time Candidates, Rebound Candidates, and Candidates of Color

I think the truth of the matter is, people who end up as "first"
don't actually set out to be first. They set out to do something
they love and it just so happens that they are the first to do it.
—Condoleezza Rice, former secretary of state

The aftermath of the 2016 election generated a new interest in politics throughout the country. This heightened interest was not only among people considering running for office but in grassroots activism and founding political organizations such as Indivisible, on the left, and Turning Point, on the right. This political environment was ripe for new candidates to emerge.[1] Throughout our research, we noted the outsized impact that Trump-era politics had on women from three demographic groups in particular: candidates running for office for the first time, women who ran in a previous election and lost and decided to run again (known as "rebound" candidates), and candidates of color. The metamorphosis experienced by some women in these groups to move from activists to political candidates has changed the landscape of electoral politics. Our research on the current political climate presents a unique opportunity to elaborate on their perspectives and experiences, which have largely been absent from the literature over the past four decades.

We wanted to understand the extent to which the national political climate influenced women in these demographic groups to run for the state legislature as well as the experiences they encountered while running. We use "(women) candidates of color" as a group when referring to Black / African American, Asian / Asian American / Pacific Islander, Hispanic/Latina, American Indian / Native American, other, and those who are multiethnic/multiracial.

Candidates Running for the First Time in 2018 and 2020

Not only did the outcome of the 2016 election have a profound impact on the number of women running at all levels of elected office, but the national political climate spurred interest in many first-time candidates running for state legislature. We were interested in knowing the extent to which female candidates, especially first-timers, were running in safe, competitive, or noncompetitive districts and whether there was evidence that the current political climate spurred women to run outside of their political comfort zone. Neither the CAWP nor the NCSL has collected data on women running for elected office for the first time at the state level. In our 2018 and 2020 national surveys, we asked respondents if they were running for state legislative office for the first time.

Our research indicates that for first-time Democrat candidates, barriers that have historically discouraged women from running were outweighed by their motivation to run in reaction to the national political climate. Measuring the intersection of the traditional barriers was important to understanding whether the first-timers were more concerned about the national political climate and less concerned about what barriers might keep them from running. Respondents in our survey conveyed the extent to which they were setting aside traditional barriers that have historically stood in the way of electoral success for women running for office in order to make a declaration about the current state of US politics. A respondent running for the first time conveyed the importance of the national political climate after 2016 regarding her decision to run:

> I initiated the process to run but was inspired at a rally on the anniversary of the women's march. I was not asked to run but was encouraged to do so when I raised my hand. (2018, Democrat, Massachusetts)

Tables 3.1 and 3.2 highlight the demographic characteristics of the respondents in 2018 and in 2020, including those who ran for the state legislature for the first time, by political party. Not surprisingly, there were more women who identified as a Democrat who were running for the first time in 2018 and in 2020, compared to their Republican counterparts. Lawless and Fox indicate that when Trump was elected, the surge in women running for Congress was highest among Democrat

TABLE 3.1. Demographic Characteristics, 2018 Surveys

	Republican	Democrat	Independent/other (missing)
Survey 1 (N = 458)			
Total	75	345	34 (4)
Race/ethnicity			
White	66	299	29
Black	1	14	0
Hispanic	1	8	0
Asian	1	6	0
Native American	1	4	1
Multiethnic/multiracial	5	13	4
Age (mean)	52.91	51.67	52.89
Running for first time (Y/N)	52/23	272/71	2/13
Survey 2 (N = 234)			
Total	34	185	12 (3)
Race/ethnicity			
White	30	168	13
Black	1	4	0
Hispanic	1	3	0
Asian	0	3	0
Native American	0	2	0
Multiethnic/multiracial	2	5	2
Age (mean)	57.00	53.49	48.65
Running for first time (Y/N)	11/23	112/73	10/5
Won in 2018 (Y/N)	20/14	74/110	0/12

TABLE 3.2. Demographic Characteristics, 2020 Survey (N = 221)

	Republican	Democrat	Independent/other (missing)
Total	56	163	0 (2)
Race/ethnicity*			
White	52	148	
Black	1	11	
Hispanic	4	8	
Asian	0	4	
Native American	0	4	
Age (mean)	53.37	51.21	
Running for first time (Y/N)	37/19	95/68	
Won in 2020 (Y/N)	28/28	62/98	
Also ran in 2018 (Y/N)	17/39	52/111	

* Some reported multiple ethnicities

women.[2] Our findings suggest that this is also the case with state legislative races. One respondent explained her reason for running this way:

> To push back against the Trump administration knowing that the state legislature was more important than ever. (2020, Democrat, Oregon)

We collected data on the extent to which the outcome of the 2016 presidential election and the current political climate in the country influenced women who were running for the first time in 2018. The question "How did you consider the following factors in your decision to run for state legislature?" was asked of these women, and table 3.3 shows an account of their responses. We ran a chi-square on these data, and the results indicate that for 2018, when considering the two measures (1) the outcome of the 2016 presidential election and (2) the current political climate in the country, there was a significant association for those who were running for the first time and for those who were Democrats. Additionally, for respondents who ran in 2020, the only significant association was with political party (Democrats) when it came to the influence of the national political climate on their decision to run. We may assume that women in our study who were running for the first time in 2020 did not feel as intense about running in 2020 as did the respondents who were running in 2018.

Despite the fact that there was not a significant association for those who were running for the first time, the national political climate was important regardless. Several of the respondents in our 2020 survey

TABLE 3.3. Factors Impacting First-Time Candidates' Decision to Run for State Legislature (Percentages)

Survey 1, 2018 (N = 458)	Outcome of the 2016 presidential election									
	Not at all important		Low importance		Neutral		Moderately important		Extremely important	
Running for first time*	Yes	No	Yes	No	Yes	No	Yes	No	Yes	No
	5.8	8.2	6.2	2.9	7.0	3.5	19.6	4.7	36	5.8
Republican	3.8	4.1	1.4	1.1	2.6	.1	0	0	0	0
Democrat**	1.4	3.2	3.8	1.7	3.5	1.7	17	4.3	33.7	5.2

	The current political climate in the country									
	Not at all important		Low importance		Neutral		Moderately important		Extremely important	
Running for first time***	Yes	No	Yes	No	Yes	No	Yes	No	Yes	No
	0	3.5	0	0	2.6	1.1	16.0	6.7	54.6	13.4
Republican	0	2.6	0	0	1.4	0	4.6	2.6	4.0	0
Democrat****	0	0	0	0	1.1	0	10.5	3.8	47.3	11.1

$\chi^2 = {}^*$ 41.10, p = .000
$\chi^2 = {}^{**}$ 109.77, p = .000
$\chi^2 = {}^{***}$ 35.84, p = .000
$\chi^2 = {}^{****}$ 75.62, p = .000

Survey, 2020 (N = 221)	What is happening in the national political scene									
	Not at all important		Low importance		Neutral		Moderately important		Extremely important	
Running for first time^	Yes	No	Yes	No	Yes	No	Yes	No	Yes	No
	0	1.3	2.3	2.8	1.8	1.8	11.9	9.6	43.0	24.0
Republican	0	0	1.8	1.0	1.0	1.0	4.1	4.1	10.0	2.7
Democrat^^	1.0	1.3	0	1.8	1.0	1.0	7.8	5.5	33.0	21.5

$\chi^2 = {}^\wedge$ 3.649, p = .456 (N.S.)
$\chi^2 = {}^{\wedge\wedge}$ 16.32, p = .003
Percentages are proportion of the total N responses to the question.

commented about how the national political climate impacted their race as well as the outcome of their race. For some respondents who ran for the first time in 2020, they were very aware of how the national political climate had trickled down to state races, and they shared their awareness about how their race was impacted by it. One respondent commented,

> I believed 2020 would be a milestone year for the Democratic Party to more accurately reflect its base by electing highly qualified, socially progressive women to office. I have always been interested in politics and the law, so I knew 2020 was a year I couldn't explain away if I didn't enter the race. I was right, I did, and I won. (2020, Democrat, New Hampshire)

Another respondent commented,

> I ran because I was outraged and infuriated by the behavior of politicians at the highest levels as well as the behavior of some people within my community. I ran because I couldn't not. I want to be able to look my grandchildren in the eye someday and tell them I did every single thing I could to help preserve and/or create a world where they could live in peace and freedom. (2020, Democrat, Arizona, lost)

First-timers were also in tune with how the national political climate influenced the outcome of their race. One respondent, when asked how she thought national and state politics impacted the outcome of her race, commented,

> Almost all Republicans in my district voted straight Republican rather than vote for individual candidates. I was promised support from the state and county political party. It was minimal primarily because they were focused almost exclusively on a high-profile US Senate race. The entire state, if not the country, was in a hyperpartisan mood. (2020, Democrat, South Carolina, lost)

There were multiple comments by respondents about how the national political climate impacted their individual state races in both 2018 and 2020. Many first-time candidates had been motivated to run by what they were witnessing nationally. At the same time, they came to discover that their own individual state legislative races could not be isolated from the effects of the national political environment.

Rebound Candidates

The CAWP reported that 15 percent of women candidates for congressional and state legislative races were likely to be rebound candidates.[3] The CAWP began documenting rebound candidates running in congressional races in 2020. There were seventy-nine women running as rebound candidates in congressional races in 2020. There is no formal documentation, yet, of the number of women rebound candidates who ran in state legislative races in 2020.

Dolan and Shah confirm that there has been little evidence about what motivates women rebound candidates to lose a campaign and want to run again.[4] They explored what motivated women rebound congressional candidates after they lost their races in the 2018 midterm election. Using data from our 2020 survey and the in-depth interviews we conducted on this unique group of state legislative candidates, we will make an attempt to fill this gap in the literature, at least temporarily.

Rebound candidates are a relatively new demographic group, and we may have Trump insurgency politics to thank for this phenomenon. Recently referred to as the new "Year of the Woman," the rebound candidates in 2020 will probably continue to run for office and shake up the electoral system.[5] Often considered a masculine approach in electoral politics, a candidate's running for office during one election cycle and losing and then running again during the following election cycle is something that has recently appealed to women congressional candidates. We saw this approach to electoral politics become an appealing option for female state legislative candidates in 2020.[6]

Our research reveals some interesting perspectives from respondents in 2020 who also ran a state legislative campaign in 2018 and lost. In our 2020 survey, there were sixty-nine respondents who reported also running in 2018, and of those respondents, thirty-seven candidates lost their 2018 races. Of these thirty-seven rebound candidates in our analysis, 17 percent of our total respondents, two of them won in 2020, and the remaining thirty-five lost their races in 2020.

Unlike the respondents in our 2020 survey who were running for the first time and for whom the national political climate may not have been a significant factor in their decision to run, the rebound candidates in 2020 overwhelmingly reported that the Trump effect was alive and well as they considered running again. Of rebound candidates whom we interviewed, four of them were Republicans, ten were Democrats, and ten mentioned that the national political climate was the reason they ran in both 2018 and 2020. Among this group of seasoned campaigners, most of them reported that they had secured more votes in 2020 than they had in 2018 and that they had narrowed the margin from their previous race, even if they lost. This group also reported seeing the national political climate (Trump, Clinton's loss in 2016, women's marches, violence around the country, Black Lives Matter) impacting their state races more in 2020 than in 2018. All of them reported being better prepared to run and being more confident candidates in 2020. A rebound candidate who lost in 2018 and in 2020 stated,

> The election of Donald Trump in 2016 is the singular reason I chose to run. I saw a danger to democracy developing, and I decided the best way to counter it would be by running locally so I could have a voice. (2020, Democrat, Indiana, lost)

Even for one Republican candidate running in an urban area in a southern state, the national political climate had both a positive and a negative impact on her campaign. She lost in 2020 by only six hundred votes, a lower margin than in 2018. She ran in 2018 after the incumbent decided to step away from the seat. She got in the race late, and with little party support, she lost. But she still decided to run again in 2020. She reported that in 2020, her opponent worked hard to destroy her reputation and that she did not plan to run again. Reacting to why she ran again in 2020, she stated,

> I felt like it was my last chance to fulfill a lifelong dream of becoming a legislator. (2020, Republican, lost)

A Democrat respondent highlighted that she was a no-name candidate in her community when she stepped up to run in 2018 but was highly motivated to run. She ultimately decided to run again in 2020 and thought that this time she would have name recognition and make some gains, which she did. She also discussed how the national political climate "very much" impacted her 2020 race. She indicated that she would not run again. She commented,

> I ran before and did well. No one had ever tried running in my area twice, and all indications were that I would continue to make gains. For me, as a local business owner, it was a win/win. My reputation is very positive in my community as a result. It definitely was a personally rewarding, growth experience. (2020, Democrat, Minnesota, lost)

A Democrat rebound respondent from Texas decided to run because a Democrat candidate had not challenged the Republican incumbent in her district since 2008. This is a sentiment we heard often from many candidates, but for the rebound candidates, they overwhelmingly reported the need to have someone running from their political party and decided that if someone else would not step up and run, they would. This respondent from Texas reported that she initiated running and stated,

> In January 2017, I made the decision to run because I was disgusted with the route that the national direction was going. (2020, Democrat, Texas, lost)

In 2018, she came within eleven hundred votes of winning and provided evidence to the party that the seat was competitive and flippable. This encouraged her to run again in 2020. She went on to say,

> I ran in 2020 because I came within eleven hundred votes of winning and thought I could win in 2020.

She indicated that she would run again (after 2020) depending on how the redistricting would play out in the coming months.

A rebound Republican candidate commented with much the same sentiment as the Democrat candidates in our study. She ran in 2018 knowing that she would lose but ran in 2020 confident that she would win. She ended up losing in 2020 but had narrowed the margin by which she lost from her 2018 campaign. Her plans at the time we interviewed her were not confirmed. She was not sure if she would run again. She stated,

> I initiated interest in 2018 when there was no Republican competition for the Democrats in my district as the filing period was closing. (2020, Republican, New Hampshire, lost)

One of the rebound candidates who decided to run in 2018 learned a lot from her last-minute decision to campaign for the seat. She lost in 2018 but won in 2020. She recounted why she ran and her experience:

> I was recruited by one past legislator, but overall, I initiated myself. I wasn't on track to run. I came out of nowhere as a candidate. [I ran] because of what's going on in the national and state level. Montana voted all red this year. In general, people were really frustrated with how our Democratic governor handled COVID and the liberal reactions to the BLM rioting. In 2018, I ran as a replacement candidate. That means I had three months to throw together a campaign. It was a great learning experience. In 2020, I was prepared and knew just what to do. (2020, Republican, Montana, won)

The pattern emerging among many rebound candidates was that their 2018 campaign was just a warm-up for them if they were not a well-known candidate. Their experiences were overall positive in 2018, and they decided that they were not ready to give up. With this momentum, they decided to keep going and run again in 2020.

While we did not set out to specifically focus on rebound candidates in our 2020 survey, we thought it was important to capitalize and report on those who responded to our survey who fit into this group. We were able to focus our efforts on this group in particular for in-depth interviews, and we interviewed fourteen of the thirty-seven rebound candidates who completed our survey. Similar to Dolan and Shah, we found that the experiences of rebound candidates in our study would fit into each of the three theoretical models they discuss: rational choice theories of political ambition (weighing the costs and benefits of a campaign), psychological theories related to losing and attributing the loss to internal or external factors, and relationally embedded models (considering how a campaign would impact them and people close to them).[7] All of the women candidates in our study touched on some aspect of each of these when debating whether to run and when assessing the outcome of their campaign. It was important for us to focus on rebound candidates and their responses as they related to the Trump effect and their decision to run.

In table 3.4, we present seven statements and responses from the 2020 survey specifically focusing on rebound candidates ($n = 37$ of the total $N = 221$). All of the statements are in response to the question "How did you consider the following factors in your decision to run for the state legislature?" These statements highlight a combination of internal and external factors. We have identified statements 1–3 as internal factors and statements 4–6 as external factors that one would consider when deciding to run for office. Statement 7 reflects the degree to which rebound candidates thought about the importance of the national political arena and its impact on their decision to run again in 2020. As you may recall, there were only two of the thirty-seven rebound candidates who won their 2020 races.

TABLE 3.4. Survey Responses from Rebound Candidates in 2020

	Not at all important		Low importance		Neutral		Moderately important		Extremely important		N/A	
	Won in 2020	Lost in 2020	Won in 2020	Lost in 2020	Won in 2020	Lost in 2020	Won in 2020	Lost in 2020	Won in 2020	Lost in 2020	Won in 2020	Lost in 2020
1. Recent desire to be in politics	0	3	1	1	0	4	0	10	1	11	0	5
2. Long-standing desire to be in politics	0	5	1	2	0	1	1	9	0	8	0	10
3. The state legislative seat was an important stepping-stone toward another higher office	2	14	0	2	0	5	0	5	0	2	0	7
4. Running for a competitive seat	0	1	0	1	0	11	0	7	2	15	0	0
5. Running in an area that generally supports the opposing party**	0	0	0	2	0	5	2	6	0	22	0	0
6. Confidence in winning the seat	0	1	0	3	0	7	1	11	1	11	0	2
7. What is happening in the national political scene*	0	0	0	0	0	2	0	8	2	25	0	0

$\chi^2 = {}^* p = .05$
$\chi^2 = {}^{**} p = .01$
Percentages are proportion of the total N responses to the question.

For the rebound candidates who lost in 2020, twenty-two of the thirty-seven respondents indicated that a recent desire to be in politics was either moderately or extremely important to them. Fewer rebound candidate respondents who lost in 2020 (seventeen of thirty-seven) indicated a long-standing desire to be in politics as moderately or extremely important to them. Interestingly, for those who lost their races in 2020, there were only slightly more respondents who indicated a recent interest in politics rather than a long-standing desire to be in politics. Perhaps reporting a long-standing desire to be in politics speaks to the persistence one needs to be a rebound candidate. On the other hand, can we assume that for these rebound candidates, the desire to run for a state legislative seat was both a recent desire due to the Trump effect and a longtime desire since they had been campaigning for two election cycles? What might we glean from the 81 percent of respondents who reported overall that this seat was an important stepping-stone toward a higher office? For some, either the idea was not applicable to them, or it was a neutral influence, or it had little to no importance with regard to higher electoral political ambitions. This finding may imply that these rebound candidates were influenced to run in 2018 and in 2020 to make any difference they could but had little interest in the state legislative seat being a stepping-stone to a higher office. This is also consistent with what these respondents conveyed to us during the in-depth interviews about why they ran in 2018 and again in 2020.

The results imply that running for a competitive seat was important for many of the respondents regardless of whether they won or lost in 2020, although eleven respondents indicated neutrality toward the statement (4). That result, coupled with the following statement about running in an area that typically supports the opposing party (5), indicates that respondents conveyed the importance of running regardless of whether they won or lost. We believe this is confirmation that these candidates felt compelled to run regardless of whether the seat was competitive and even if they perceived that the other party might win. They did not want the race to be void of representatives from either major party. The results for the statement that follows about one's confidence in winning the seat (6) suggests that these rebound candidates were confident about winning the seat and that this was important in their decision to run again in 2020. Many of these candidates had made significant strides in 2018 regarding the seat and believed that they had an opportunity to win the seat in 2020 regardless of whether they were running for a competitive seat in an area that would typically support the opposing party. These results coincide with what these candidates conveyed to us: they would rather run and lose than leave the seat open, and they were motivated by the strides they had made in 2018 and had more confidence in a successful campaign.

We included the last statement about the national political climate to convey the importance of what was going on around the nation as this group of rebound candidates contemplated running again in 2020. Of the rebound candidate respondents, 95 percent indicated that the national political climate was moderately or extremely important to their decision to run in 2020 regardless of whether they won or lost.

All of the women we interviewed in this group who reported losing in 2020 indicated that they would stay involved with their party or with assisting other campaigns, especially if they did not intend to run again. All reported that they learned a great deal from their campaigns, and many reported that they would run again. For those who commented that they would not be running again, their experiences had a psychologically negative impact on them, even though they attributed the outcome of their race to external factors (negative ads, voter turnout, national-level politics overshadowing their races) rather than to internal factors (competence, skill set, campaign experience). Vallejo suggests that the attribution of external factors to electoral failure is often a masculine assessment of a campaign outcome.[8] Male electoral candidates often attribute their campaign success to internal rather than external factors. Our findings suggest that women rebound candidates attributed the outcome of their race more to external factors rather than to internal factors, thus suggesting more confidence in pursuing consecutive campaigns.

Candidates of Color

In 1924, the first woman of color and the first Native American woman, Cora Belle Reynolds Anderson, was elected to serve in the Michigan state legislature. In 1928, the first Black woman, Minnie Buckingham Harper, was appointed to the West Virginia state legislature. Two years later, two Latina women were elected to serve in the New Mexico legislature, Fedelina Lucero Gallegos and Porfiria Hidalgo Saiz. The first Black woman elected to a state legislature was Crystal Dreda Bird Fauset in 1938.[9]

The number of women candidates of color running for state legislatures has incrementally increased by small margins over the past twenty-five years. African American women in state legislatures continue to maintain the largest proportion of women of color serving at that level. After the 1996 general election, there were 232 women of color elected to serve in a state legislative seat, and after the 2020 general election, the number serving was 552.[10]

Figure 3.1 shows the incremental increase in women of color serving in state legislatures. This information was retrieved from the CAWP, and the first year it records for women of color securing state legislative seats is 1996.[11] Juenke et al. estimate that candidates of color will be represented in Congress in equal proportion to their percentage in the population in 2050.[12] In 2019, women of color made up 20.3 percent of the population.[13] Currently, women of color make up only 7.5 percent of all state legislative seats. At this rate, women of color would need a 200 percent increase in state legislative seats to barely exceed the current percentage of women of color in the population. By 2050, the demographic trends in the US are projected to reflect a more diverse population. Will we see more women of color in electoral politics? Juenke et al. indicate that trends in state legislature representation predict what the future demographic of Congress will look like.[14] If this is the case, can we expect to see much of the same slow progress in representatives of color both in state legislatures and in Congress, or will the Trump effect accelerate this progress?

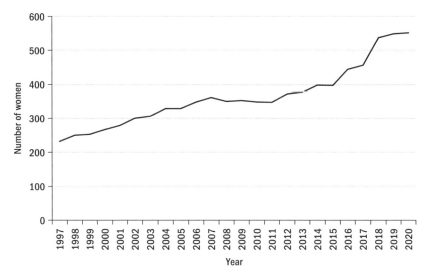

FIGURE 3.1. Progression of women of color serving in state legislatures from 1996 to 2021 (Data from Center for American Women and Politics, 2020b)

In figure 3.2, you can easily visualize the percentage of women of color serving in state legislatures when compared to all state legislators and women state legislators. In 1996, the percentage of women of color serving in state legislatures was 3.1 percent. The percentage doubled to 7.5 percent after the 2020 general election.[15] During the same time period, the percentage of women state legislators who were women of color increased from 14.3 percent in 1996 to 25.5 percent in 2021.

Most women candidates of color are Democrats, and women of color make up more than 35 percent of state legislative Democrat candidates. Women of color make up less than 10 percent of all Republican candidates. It makes sense that when there is a Democrat blue wave across the country, the number of candidates of color elected to serve increases. Similar to the overall assessment of gender, when women run, they tend to win as often as their male counterparts do. The same is true for candidates of color: when they run, they win as often as other candidates do when running in districts that favor their party and when their party recruits and supports them.[16]

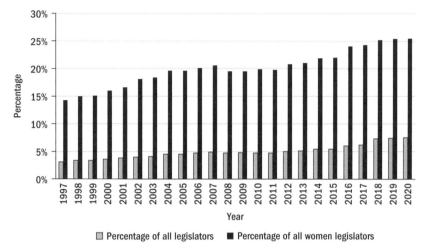

FIGURE 3.2. Percentage of women of color serving in the state legislature (Data from Center for American Women and Politics, 2020b)

In 2020, there was a woman of color serving in every state legislature except for in Nebraska. And if you are a woman of color with political ambition, the place to reside and run may be New Mexico, which is among the six states that have the highest percentage of women of color serving in the state legislature but is the leading state for women of color serving in executive statewide office. New Mexico may be the most promising state for women of color in electoral politics because of its history of electing women of color and encouragement by the national organization Emerge to recruit women of diverse backgrounds to run for office.[17]

Our results are consistent with what has been reported in the literature about the emergence of women candidates of color in electoral politics: their experiences and advocacy influence public policy, and their involvement in grassroots organizations shape their preparedness and confidence to run and serve.[18] One respondent recounted why she ran:

I decided to run because it was a childhood dream. After a close friend who was a fierce advocate for women in politics died on the heels of the 2016 election, I was motivated to revisit my own dreams and run for office. I looked around and didn't like what I saw, and I thought we needed more women to run and win. (2020, African American, won)

Another respondent described her experience with the party, which discouraged her from running. Her experience emphasizes that women of color have a disproportionately harder time challenging the power that well-established parties may have over who moves forward and runs for a seat.[19] Carroll and Sanbonmatsu point out that we may not see an increase in candidates of color that reflects their numbers in the population because they do not receive the same level of recruitment or support from the party to run.[20] One respondent discussed her experience with the party and the support she received:

> I initiated and was discouraged by people in power but persisted anyway. I received invaluable support by a grassroots organization that had no ties to the established power structure in place. Eventually two key people who were connected to the establishment decided to give me advice and encouragement behind the scenes. We went from a long shot to a toss-up! (2018, Hispanic, Democrat, running for the first time)

What we found supports the notion that when women of color run, they have a high likelihood of winning their race, especially when supported by their party. One of the reasons that this may be the case is that they are often running in majority-minority districts.[21] About 11 percent of the women who responded to our surveys in 2018 were candidates of color. For the 2020 survey, 14.4 percent of the women who responded were candidates of color. In 2018, 14 percent of respondents who were candidates of color were running for the first time, and in 2020, 17.4 percent of respondents who were candidates of color reported running for the first time. For the twenty-two candidates of color responding to the postelection survey in 2018, thirteen of them won their races, and six of the thirteen who won their races were running for the first time. For the thirty-two candidates of color responding to the 2020 survey, twenty-two of them won their races, and eight out of twenty-two who won their races were running for the first time. Respondents of color who were running for the first time reported being recruited to run for state legislative office:

> I was recruited by a congressional candidate in my district. (2018, African American, Colorado)

> [I was] recruited. I was approached to run for the seat a few times but declined. It wasn't until the night before that I was approached again and made the final decision to run. (2018, Asian American)

> I was recruited by a neighbor to run. (2018, African American)

> I was recruited by legislative friends. (2018, African American)

> I was recruited by the county party chair. (2018, Hispanic/Latina)

> [I was] recruited. People had asked me for a long time if I would ever run for office, and while I thought I might do this toward the end of my current career, I didn't feel qualified. After the election of 2016, several people asked me to consider running for the particular seat I am seeking. (2018, Hispanic/Latina, Colorado)

Other respondents in our study reported initiating the process to run, citing the importance of running as well as taking the steps necessary to move their candidacy forward. It is common for candidates of color, especially women, to take atypical recruitment pathways to running.[22] Two candidates of color stated,

> I initiated the process of running because I thought it was important for a new and different voice to be added to the legislature. (2018, African American, Maryland)

I initiated [running] and contacted local state representatives for guidance. (2018, African American)

Respondents of color who initiated the process of running reported a mixed bag when it came to their experiences. Their accounts support both positively and negatively the aspects of party power and party support. One respondent's experience suggests that the party was supportive of her candidacy at the state level. She commented,

> I initiated the process to run for county commissioner, and a county party representative suggested I run for state house. (2018, African American)

Another respondent experienced what reflects a lack of support, even though she won her race. She stated,

> I was informally recruited by some friends, but there was no "formal" recruitment, especially because I ran against an eighteen-year Democrat incumbent in a safe blue district. (2020, African American)

Another respondent, who had a very positive experience with being recruited, stated,

> Someone reached out to me. I've attended a variety of political trainings over the years through different organizations, but I was always on the fence about running. When I got into politics on the advocacy side, I told myself I would never run for this particular race. I got a call from a local elected official (white male) who thought I would be great and listed all the reasons including more women representation and people of color. I told him I would pray about it, and the rest is history. (2020, African American, won)

Similar to other professions and industries, individuals contemplating electoral politics need to see representatives who look like them in order to consider running themselves.[23] One respondent expressed this idea when she stated,

> Current representatives are far-right, conservative, elderly, straight men and had never been challenged by the left before. I wanted to see myself reflected in my representatives, and the only way that was going to happen was to run myself. (2020, Hispanic/Latina, lost)

Another respondent made a similar comment about why she ran:

> The desire to work for the common good. The need for representation by a working person of color. (2020, Hispanic/Latina, lost)

The desire and necessity to see yourself in the representation of others around you is especially important when it comes to politics; however, it continues to lag. As we see more historically red states elect Democrat congressional candidates of color who flip the state from red to blue, such as what we observed in Georgia in January 2021, will this trickle down to state legislative races so that more candidates of color, particularly women, get elected? Silva and Skulley suggest that more candidates of color running in a previous election will positively correspond to the number running in a future election cycle.[24] If this finding holds true, we should continue to see incremental increases in the number of women running for and securing state legislative seats. Does this mean, however, that this increase will be realized only in districts with political identity strongholds? One respondent who was running as an incumbent but had flipped the seat in 2018 stated,

> Democrats are severely in the minority in the Florida legislature. I wanted to run in a seat that would help bring more balance to the legislature. I flipped a seat from red to blue in 2018 and was able to run unopposed this cycle. It is a competitive swing seat. Last, I wanted to run and win

because we need more women and especially women of color in the Florida legislature. (2020, Democrat, Florida, won)

Women candidates of color confront similar barriers as other women (family/caregiving responsibilities and how professional background and skill sets play into running for office), but they also confront additional barriers when running for office. Female candidates of color, in particular, not only encounter gender-related barriers to running for office but also face barriers associated with racial bias. Many of our respondents confirmed additional barriers to running that their counterparts may not have to consider when contemplating running, as well as barriers that they experience throughout the process, especially amid the Black Lives Matter movement. One respondent commented,

Being a woman of color in a majority-white state is hard. I think I have had a harder time with people assuming that because I'm a Black woman, I must be a single mother or that I live in the poorer part of town. I only had any "respect" or acknowledgment when I told people that I'm a veteran. It sucks that that was the way I had to earn acceptance. I'll probably run as an independent next time. (2018, Democrat, running for the first time)

One respondent discussed how being a candidate of color positively impacted the outcome of her race, particularly because of Black Lives Matter:

I believe that being a woman and being a person of color were immensely important in my run. With the rise in women running for office and the political momentum around the George Floyd killing, I think people wanted to give a woman of color a chance to lead. I think my professional experience [lawyer, diversity and inclusion professional] sealed the deal. My primary opponent was a white male lawyer, and as one constituent said, "If you both have the same qualifications, why *shouldn't* I choose the woman of color over the status quo?" (2020, Democrat, Minnesota, won)

In the summer of 2020, throughout the country and across the world, George Floyd, Breonna Taylor, and additional cases of racial injustice further fueled the Black Lives Matter movement, which was sparked after George Zimmerman was acquitted in 2013 in the 2012 shooting death of Trayvon Martin.[25] Several reports during 2020 suggested that the Black Lives Matter movement and a broader awareness of systemic racism would have a profound impact on the results of the general election in November.[26] To what extent was the Black Lives Matter movement ultimately a political force? Kaplan stated in a report in the *American Prospect*, "the powerful moral idea behind Black Lives Matter has officially become a mainstream political force at precisely the moment that the Democrats, all of us, really needed one."[27]

As it turns out, the Black Lives Matter movement had a profound impact on the outcome of the general election in 2020, getting a record number of voters to register and vote, which eventually secured 53 percent of the vote for Biden/Harris and 46 percent for Trump/Pence. The battleground states of Pennsylvania and Georgia helped to elect Joe Biden, and in January 2021, the Senate went to the Democrats when the races were finalized in Georgia.[28] There is little doubt that the Black Lives Matter movement will continue to influence electoral politics and prospective candidates running at all levels.[29] The question going forward is whether we will continue to see the momentum created by the protests and the values reflected in the Black Lives Matter movement result in an increasing number of electoral candidates of color, particularly women, in the upcoming election cycles. If the answer is yes, we should see an increase, more than has been typical, in the number of women candidates of color running for state legislatures.

Conclusion

In this chapter, we have put a limelight on three demographic groups that deserve their own chapter in a book focused on Trump-era politics. It would have been ideal to have historical data available about first-time legislative and rebound candidates to know the extent to which the political climate since 2016 increased the number of women running who identify with these groups. Our findings suggest that the current political climate was moderately or extremely important for 54 percent of first-time legislative candidates in 2018 who had no previous experience in electoral politics. Of respondents in 2018, 62 percent indicated that they were running for the first time for a state legislative seat. This suggests that the national political climate was quite influential to this group as they considered running for a state legislative seat. This is certainly an aspect of political ambition with regard to first-time candidates that deserves further study. As future election cycles are studied, it will be important to observe the trends among first-time female legislative candidates and to consider the extent to which they shy away from state legislative races as their entry point into electoral politics or choose to run in gateway elected positions that would eventually lead them to a state legislative race.

Our findings with regard to rebound candidates indicate that after two subsequent races, while some may not intend to run again, they do intend to stay involved. Perhaps the Trump effect has had a positive impact on women rebound candidates (especially those in our research) because they have developed more confidence and have begun to attribute their electoral failure to external factors rather than to internal factors, which may positively influence their political ambition.

The notion that being a rebound candidate is a masculine approach to electoral politics may be debunked as we see an increase in women rebound candidates in future election cycles. Perhaps the phenomenon of women rebound candidates is only a result of Trump insurgency politics and will decrease in future election cycles. This certainly is a phenomenon to observe and quantify so that we can better understand the conditions that contribute to the number of women rebound candidates from one election cycle to the next. It remains to be seen whether the Trump effect was merely a fluke or a positive by-product of a political condition that will result in keeping more women politically engaged across multiple election cycles.

Perry indicates that candidates of color have a higher likelihood of being elected in areas or districts that also have a higher proportion of people of color.[30] The notion of identity politics plays in favor of candidates of color when they represent a similar constituency. However, is this the only path into electoral politics for women candidates of color? It may not be the only path, but it is one path that needs to be considered, especially where there are few or no representatives of color serving constituents in areas with a large minority demographic makeup. Women of color who have a desire to run for state legislative office should consider running especially if they reside in districts that have a demographic composition with more residents of color. The pipeline to winning is not simply running but party support that fosters an environment for women of color to run.[31] Not only might an entrance into electoral politics for women of color be the glass ceiling that they need to shatter, but they also need a level of perseverance that their white counterparts may not need in order to seek office.[32]

4

Running for State Legislature

A Complex Web of Factors

I've never been a planner. I didn't know I was going to run for
the state house. I didn't know I was going to run for governor.
I don't know what's next, and I love not thinking about it because the doors open at a certain time.
—Nikki Haley, first female governor of South Carolina

With the decision to run in the rearview mirror, women running
for the state legislature, in 2018 and 2020, were ready to confront the
national political climate head-on. We tried to capture the entire campaign experience of female candidates, ranging from the strategies and
tactics they employed to the impact that the Trump effect had on the
decisions they made. This approach provided an opportunity to better
understand the ways women run in the complex web of electoral and
party politics. The pandemic that hit early in 2020 added an unexpected and difficult layer to what was already a challenging political
environment. Through it all, survey respondents demonstrated that
they possessed the appropriate skill set to campaign effectively in a
politically volatile environment as well as when confronted with the
unforeseen challenges presented by COVID-19.

Jumping into a Hostile Political Climate

Hyperpartisanship, or party sorting, pushes voters into two camps.[1]
The results of the 2018 midterm election and the 2020 general election
reinforced the sorting theory. In 2018, despite energy from the #MeToo

movement and the women's marches, Democrats were only able to improve their standing in six state legislatures. In 2020, an expected down-ballot "blue wave" never materialized.[2] Democrats lost seats in the House and narrowly took control of the Senate. Very little changed at the state level, where Republicans held their own in down-ballot races. A higher-than-expected turnout by voters in rural areas was a key factor in ebbing the blue wave.[3] Joe Biden had won a critical presidential election for the Democratic Party, yet down ballot, the political winds had barely changed.

Enter into the mix a global pandemic, a resulting economic crisis, and a series of racial injustices, and an even more complex political environment emerged as the 2020 campaign season unfolded. Perhaps looking to make sense of this cloudy situation, there was evidence that party sorting helped Americans to cope. For instance, reactions to the pandemic quickly broke along partisan lines. Republicans were less likely to embrace wearing a mask than Democrats were.[4] Republicans viewed the economy as their most important issue, while Democrats listed the pandemic as their major concern.[5] Simultaneously, Democrats were demanding police reform as one way to address social injustice, while Republicans expressed worry over defunding the police.[6] It is against this backdrop that we surveyed women running for the state legislature over two major election cycles.

In 2020, respondents conveyed that many conversations between candidates and voters often hinged on the answer to a simple question: "Are you for or against Trump?" One Democrat candidate from a Mountain West state, who engaged in COVID-era socially distanced door-to-door campaigning, mentioned experiencing many Trump-focused conversation starters or, perhaps more accurately, conversation stoppers:

> A lot of voters asked me who I would vote for and said they would not vote for me if I didn't vote for Trump. (2020, Democrat, Mountain West state, suburban, won)

Another Democrat anticipated the Trump effect having a positive influence on their get-out-the-vote efforts. While the strategy may have been successful in reaching Democratic Party voters, she noted that the Trump effect cut both ways:

> We actually tied a lot of our marketing to it. All the polling had shown how unpopular Trump was. [The message] worked in [Democratic] areas but not in [other] areas in the district. So many voters had already made up their minds. It was a case of the die having been cast a lot sooner than we had thought. (2020, Democrat, lost)

This candidate's unsuccessful bid against a female Republican is a good example of the Trump effect having a negative impact on a Democratic Party hopeful in 2020. She stated,

> Trump supporters had the biggest impact on my race. Over six thousand voters showed up and voted Republican, more than ever before in the district.

A Republican candidate, running for the first time in 2020, conveyed how the Trump effect impacted the outcome of her state legislative race in a majority-Democrat district. Although she lost in two consecutive elections, the Trump effect actually helped her close the gap. She explained,

> Republican women in this area lost by huge numbers in 2018. [In 2020] I lost by seven points and was told I would lose by twenty. [The Republican Party] focused on national issues, and we needed to focus on local residents, and they obviously did not. One hundred percent [it was the Trump effect]. I was interviewed numerous times after the election, and basically, I know that from talking to people, I lost to the hatred of Donald Trump in my region. I even heard this among Republicans. (2020, Republican, Northeast tri-state region, lost)

Another Republican, from a competitive district in Ohio, recognized that the Trump effect might work against her in a suburban district. She focused instead on her long-established presence in the community:

> I have broad support in my district and with reaching out to both sides. The [Republican Party] had a campaign, but I did all my stuff locally. I want to live in this community. This is your reputation and legacy. (2020, Republican, Ohio, won)

Trump was not on the ballot in 2018, but you would not have known it by the comments of some of the respondents. When asked, "What factors do you think most impacted your state legislative race?" one Republican candidate who ran in 2018 linked her defeat to the Trump effect:

> The Trump effect—which created unprecedented turnout in our district and state. They were voting Democratic because of their hatred of Trump even though I ran on my own platform. (2018, Republican, Pennsylvania, lost)

Another 2018 Republican candidate commented,

> People believed all Republicans to be the same. A vote against me was a vote against Trump. (2018, Republican, Pennsylvania, lost)

Conversely, several Democrat candidates thought they benefited from the Trump factor as they campaigned in 2018:

> Anti-Trump sentiment, concern about the divisiveness in America, wanting to elect moderates who will talk to one another. (2018, Democrat, New Hampshire, won)

> People were displeased with the hate politics Trump stirred up. (2018, Democrat, New Hampshire, won)

President Trump's fear mongering about the caravan. No question. (Democrat, 2018, Massachusetts, won)

However, one respondent was not so pleased to discover that Trump was a factor in a nonpresidential election cycle:

Trump confusing voters that he was on the ballot was a huge distraction from any other message. (2018, Democrat, Pennsylvania, lost)

The following rebound candidate discussed her take on the Trump effect across two election cycles. In 2018, the Democrat had an uphill battle running against a longtime incumbent who in the past often had run unopposed. Nevertheless, the national political climate motivated her to run, and her efforts resulted in a markedly increased turnout. To her credit, she fell just short of victory, losing by a mere 1.4 percent. Because of her unexpected close call in 2018, the district was considered flippable in 2020. However, in 2020, turnout surged among Republican as well as Democrat voters. Despite more resources thrown into what was thought to be a flippable seat, she again fell short of victory, but this time by a slightly greater margin of 2.4 percent. She explained in more detail what occurred:

The conventional wisdom that presidential election voters would come out for Democrats was true, but the Trump side was really fired up. On Election Day, Trump signs and Trump voters were everywhere on the street corners. [Throughout the campaign] I tried to stay away from national politics. My argument was local politics is not the same as national politics. So I tried to stay out of the national frenzy. But I had no illusions that anyone who supported Trump was ever going to vote for me. (2020, Democrat, Massachusetts, lost)

Another Democrat female candidate found herself on the receiving end of negative imagery that tied her to a different national political figure, Speaker of the US House of Representatives Nancy Pelosi, who was a favorite target of Republicans and President Trump during the Trump era. She stated the following:

> Well, all of the negative pieces my opponent did, none of it was just about me. They were all about me being Nancy Pelosi's puppet. Voting for me was like voting for Pelosi. Everything was about national Democratic policies. One TV ad was showing me and Nancy in the same outfits. We knew we would put [the opponent] in an awkward position because I was known in the community as a community leader who [helped] people, was involved with homeless shelters, all of these sorts of things. (2020, Democrat, suburban, Minnesota, won)

The national attention paid to a US Senate race stood out for another respondent as a major factor in the outcome of her race:

> It was all about the nationalization of the Lindsay Graham versus Jaime Harrison Senate race. Voter turnout and a red wave. (2020, Democrat, South Carolina, lost)

One respondent was fully cognizant that she was running in a gerrymandered Republican district but apparently hoped that the national political climate would shift her way after four years of President Trump's brand of conservatism:

> We are a gerrymandered district; however, I thought voters would not support Donald Trump and Republican candidates. I guess I was wrong. In spite of all the horrible things Republicans and Donald Trump stood for, they still voted the same way. (2020, Democrat, Pennsylvania, lost)

The comments of respondents across two election cycles suggest a growing Trump effect. Democratic Party campaigns were buoyed by anti-Trump sentiment in both 2018 and 2020. However, by 2020, a growing, substantial, and immovable pro-Trump constituency appeared to be far more impactful on the campaign trail than in 2018. In this environment, respondents expressed frustration that state legislative races were so tied to national politics. As one respondent stated,

> I spoke with many voters who asked me about issues that I couldn't deal with as a state legislator. They were things, such as immigration or "the wall," that I had no control over. (Democrat, 2020, lost)

Ways Women Run

We know that when women decide to run for office, they win at roughly the same rate as men. This reality suggests a similar campaign experience for both men and women.[7] In this vein, we wanted to learn more about what female candidates were doing as campaigners in the Trump-era political climate. To accomplish this task, we asked respondents to reflect on a variety of questions related to their campaign experience. Did you participate in professional training programs, especially those geared for women? Did you receive adequate party support? Did you experience any situations while campaigning when you thought you were being singled out as a woman, either positively or negatively? In analyzing the responses, it became apparent that messaging was of critical importance to understanding the ways women were campaigning. Studies on the use of social media reveal that female candidates focus more on hope in their messages, while men are more likely to rely on language of anger and disgust.[8] One theme that stood out among respondents was their insistence on presenting a positive message to voters, sometimes over the objections of their party or campaign staff. Also noteworthy was the frustration that some Democrat respondents expressed about their party's overall message, which was seen as too complicated and layered to sell to voters, as opposed to more simplistic and straightforward sound bites coming from the Republican side.

The Value of Professional Development Opportunities

One way candidates may prepare to run for office is through professional development programs. There are many offerings to choose from, ranging from national, state, local, partisan, and bipartisan programs. Among respondents, professional development programs were generally well received. Here is one example of a respondent extolling the benefit of campaign training provided explicitly for women.

> Having training is vital. We have several excellent candidate training programs here in Hawaii. They provide a comprehensive overview of everything you need from messaging to fundraising. The number-one thing I recommend for all women running is to take a training course on how to run for office. (2020, Democrat, Hawaii, won)

The potential benefits of participating in candidate training programs can go beyond simply learning about how to do fundraising or developing a message. One respondent stated,

> The Network of Exceptional Women, consultants from Seattle, and Emerge Washington provided training. Women aren't always self-identifying, so the networking is important. [It was] about learning how to create and find female candidates. (2020, Democrat, Washington State, lost)

A first-time female candidate felt she was operating from an isolated island until she reached out and attended a national campaign training conference. She shared her experience:

> If you're a woman running for the first time, you essentially are mandated to participate in a training program. I needed that, as I didn't know what the hell I was doing. So I showed up for every opportunity I could find and soaked it up as much as possible. But in Texas, I felt like a little blue dot in a sea of red. There was nothing specifically for women, and I felt isolated,

ignorant, and helpless. So I attended the national P triple C training [Progressive Campaign Committee for Change]. I walked into a room of three hundred people who felt just like me. And we were all there because we were all worried about the country and everyone's future. We found each other, and it was the best, most soulful experience I ever had because I was able to find comradery and realized I am not alone. It was so reassuring. I was able to network with these people over four days of sessions and dinners with new friends in the evenings. There were sessions on all aspects of campaigning including fundraising and messaging. It included a session on how women have to walk a fine line and that we will be criticized more heavily than a man and strategies to deal with it. While they addressed your appearance, it was more about awareness than insisting you be a certain way. And so, when I left, I not only felt I had found my people, but I felt my chains were off. I was confident in where I was going. (2020, Democrat, Texas, lost)

This respondent was running in a noncompetitive district; nevertheless, she took it upon herself to find other avenues to help keep motivated in a race that she was destined to lose. Another candidate, also running in a noncompetitive district, conveyed frustration that the party had little or no interest in training her to become a more effective candidate:

This is a very Republican district. It is extremely rare for a Democrat to win here. I think my race was the most competitive in the county [lost with 42 percent of the vote]. I could have won if I knew how to properly campaign. I wasted so much time trying to figure out the basics of what I needed to do and how to do it. This district could be won with someone who actually knows how to campaign. I didn't have access to VoteBuilder—the website tells who the voters are, which party, and their voting history. After early voting, I had no way to target those who had not yet turned in their ballot. I asked for this information from some of the larger campaigns, but they did not have time to help me. Every Democrat here thinks they are the only one. They feel so isolated because there is no infrastructure here. (2020, Democrat, Utah, lost)

Another respondent conveyed a similar story:

> I had mostly moral support. I did attend a one-day workshop on fund-raising. I was not a top-tier candidate so probably did not have the support a tier one would get. (2020, Democrat, Georgia, lost)

The cost of training as well as the time commitment was impactful for another respondent:

> The party provided no support for me to attend a training program. I had to pay for it out of my own funds. Cost along with the time commitment were prohibitive. (2020, Democrat, lost)

One respondent dispensed with campaign training, confident that her executive-level credentials were a good fit for running a campaign. She was also in a good position for party support as the district was identified by the party as flippable. She stated,

> I had extensive executive leadership training at [the corporate level] and a campaign manager with experience who knew who to contact to get things done. There were two entities involved, the Assembly Democratic Committee and the state Democratic Party. This was a race they wanted to win. The party had check-ins on a regular basis. I would give my wants, and [the party] would respond since I might win. (2020, Democrat, Wisconsin, won by 1.5 percent margin)

Several respondents saw value in helping women learn the ropes of how to campaign and in developing a support network but raised broader concerns about the goals and objectives of such programs. One stated,

> A main reason to attend training programs is it's a great networking opportunity. But it also sucks up a lot of time. [One program] was led by men and started off with "what women wear makes men sweat." The

training that needs to happen, it's not for women. It needs to be for men. There is a ridiculous amount of misogyny out there. It's men that need to learn how to behave. (2020, Democrat, Iowa, won)

Another respondent commented that providing training for state legislative candidates is an important step toward building the party and grooming candidates for higher office:

The national Democratic Party needs to support state races and start growing candidates for the future of the Democratic Party. Just like major league baseball has the minor leagues, the state legislative candidates should be supported and developed so they can later be drafted for other roles. (2018, Democrat, northern Great Plains state, lost)

Important questions were raised by respondents regarding the goals of campaign training geared for women. What are the outcomes that these programs are trying to achieve? Are they simply to provide training on how to campaign? Or is a primary purpose of training programs to be somehow uniquely beneficial for women? As long as there is a sense that the "good old boy's network" persists in politics, there will be a need for training geared toward women.[9] Our research reveals that for some respondents, good intentions have fallen short of changing the landscape in which women run for office. Yet, respondents found it helpful in alleviating some of the anxieties associated with the nuts and bolts of campaigning as well as in building a support network with other women running for office. Both major parties could be doing more to support female candidates; however, more states have functioning pipelines to female Democrats than to Republicans.[10]

Resources: Political Party and Securing Financial Support

We noted earlier in this chapter the story of a female Republican state legislative candidate in Ohio who distanced herself from the national political scene and focused instead on her personal ties to the district. In a two-party system, we tend to generalize Democrats and Republicans as monolithic entities whose principles are straightforward and uniformly shared. The reality is that candidates engage with multiple actors from within and outside the party who are not always on the same page. Outside the party, supposed allies such as political action committees (PACs) also frame the identities of Republican and Democrat candidates.[11] In this reality, one respondent spoke to the complex environment of running under her party label:

> The Democratic establishment manipulated the legislature, gave zero help, and even attacked me in numerous ways. This explains why there has to be a new crop of recruits in each election because this pattern of unethical behavior and actions cause recruits not to run again due to the damage emotionally and financially these establishment entities cause. (2018, Democrat, Maryland)

Another respondent believed both parties to be out of touch with what motivates women interested in running for office. She commented,

> I do not think either of the two parties respond to women's needs. They are responding to the big, rich corporate sponsor needs and the arrogance and greed of their inner circle, clinging to their positions. Hillary and Nancy Pelosi are old white women clinging to power just like Mitch McConnell. Women are rising mainly on their own. (2018, Libertarian Party, Mountain West state)

Some candidates had to consider whether to carve out their own campaign as distinctive from statewide party politics. A Democrat running "down-state" from Chicago described her situation this way:

> Party politics in Illinois are complicated, particularly in central and southern areas of the state where being labeled a "Chicago Democrat" is

difficult to overcome. For that reason, I didn't seek much support from our state party. It worked to my advantage to show swing voters in my district that I was an independent-minded candidate with a locally run campaign. I'm not sure how much support I would have received if I had sought it out. We also don't have particularly strong county Democratic Parties in central and southern Illinois. One of the counties I will represent has been much more helpful than the other, but that's only because the other county lacks the membership, infrastructure, and experience to help. (2018)

Party leadership makes tough decisions regarding the prioritization and distribution of resources in order to maximize the odds of statewide electoral success. Factors such as the competitiveness of the district, incumbency, whether the race is an open seat, and the quality of each candidate determine how the party allocates funds and staff support.[12] In short, more money will typically be poured into seats considered most likely to secure majority control of the state legislature. Nevertheless, parties are not infallible in their assessments of where to spend resources. A candidate from 2018 discussed frustration over the party determining in advance that her seat would not be competitive:

The race from the beginning was considered not a viable race. I received minimal support from my local Democratic Party, zero from the House Democratic Party, and zero from the state party. I proved that this is possible with more help and resources. The politicking that goes on within our own party is shameful. I came within 1,500 votes in a district that has a 7,500+R advantage. I can only imagine what could have been with a little help. (Democrat)

Over time, one rebound candidate and her party learned to accommodate each other's perspectives on how best to campaign. Here is how she described the evolution of her campaigns over two election cycles:

In 2018, we were actually discouraged from using social media because [the party argued] you can't translate it into statistics to use next time. I focused on grassroots efforts and social media more than others did. If you raise a lot of money, the party gets excited about your campaign. One of the things that was really important to me personally was my motto to avoid conflict and negative campaigning. And the way things go negative is you raise a lot of money. If you raise a lot of money, all of these other entities take stock in your campaign. I wanted to make sure I had very little money. So it was absolutely important to me that I did everything different than you were supposed to. But I did things differently. As a result, there was no negative campaigning. I had a conversation with my opponent, and I said, "If I can do it, you can do it." So we agreed. The community stepped in and didn't do it either. I stayed positive, and though we didn't win either time, that part, in my opinion, was a success because we stayed positive. Yet I felt I had 100 percent party support, though I did not meet their qualifications of how to campaign. They made exceptions for me. I didn't have the x amount of dollars or x number of calls or x number of doors knocked. They went ahead and threw support my way, assigning staff and direct access to other resources. They did all of that anyway in both years. The one thing I would have done in 2020, if not for COVID, was more door knocking. For my race, [the party] recognized the value of what I was bringing to try and get elected. They threw out the standard playbook and stuck by me 100 percent. (2020, Democrat, Minnesota, lost in 2018 and 2020)

Another respondent talked about running to replace the incumbent from her party who had decided to retire. She painted him as more of a centrist and thought the district, 60 percent Democrat, was ready for a more progressive candidate. Although running in a safe district, she hoped for more from the party. She stated,

The party support was okay. They said I'd get 100 percent, but I felt like I was getting only 10 percent. Sometimes they were quick to do media ads, which was helpful. (2020, Democrat, Minnesota, suburban, won)

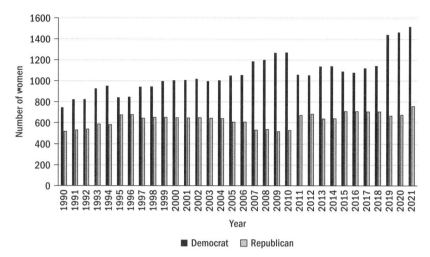

FIGURE 4.1. Number of women state legislators from 1990 to 2021, by political party (Data from Center for American Women and Politics, 2020b)

Far fewer women run for the state legislature under the Republican label compared to the Democratic Party. From 1981 through 1995, the gap between the state legislative seats held by Democrat women and Republican women was fairly narrow. From that point onward, the number of Democrat female state legislators has grown significantly, while the number of Republican females has remained relatively flat (see figure 4.1).

One explanation for the difference holds that as the Republican Party shifted further to the right, less attention was given to recruiting female candidates.[13] The Republican Party appears to have focused on conservative values rather than the sex/gender of their messengers.[14] Culturally, Republicans tend to reject identity politics.[15] This perspective, it is argued, has discouraged Republican women from running. The struggles for Republican women begin early on in the recruitment process. Candidates, both male and female, receive little financial support during the primary stage of the campaign process.[16]

This gender-blind recruiting environment has made it more difficult for Republican women to raise money to compete during primaries, when donor sources are far more fragmented.[17] Simply, the lack of awareness and limited scope of Republican political action committees has put Republican female candidates at a disadvantage. In a survey of conservative women, 72 percent of them had never heard of PACs set up to assist women running as Republican candidates. In contrast, 93 percent of progressive women were aware of PACs that supported women candidates.[18] In this regard, Emily's List raised $45 million for female Democrat candidates, whereas Maggie's List secured only $210,000 for conservative candidates in 2016.[19] One Democrat respondent commented on how important she thought an endorsement by Emily's List would have been in the race she lost:

> I wish I had been endorsed by a group such as Emily's List. I think it mattered in two other races where candidates won in my state. (2018, Democrat, lost)

Another respondent echoed the potential barriers to women running as Republicans. A candidate from a red state commented that her party was doing very little to recruit women to run. The party simply relies on candidates to step forward. She explained,

> I don't see recruitment efforts on the Republican side. I do see on the Democratic side a huge push to recruit women. I think [the Republican Party] just looks for the most qualified candidate instead of really looking to gender. I just don't think there is much effort on the Republican side. It's just a matter of deciding to run. Maybe it's because we are such a red state. We don't screen candidates, and we are maybe seeing more fighting within the party as a result. So you are pretty much on your own when you decide to run. (2020, Republican, Great Plains state, urban district, lost)

More broadly speaking, another female Republican candidate noted that, in her experiences talking to female Republican voters, they were not always supportive of women running:

Republican women don't support each other. We are our own worst critics. (2020, Republican, Northeast tri-state area, lost)

We noted one Republican female candidate who bumped up against a male primary opponent who not only attacked her directly in mailers and television ads but also benefited from a PAC that ran attack ads against her. At the same time, independent-expenditure PACs ran ads on her behalf during the primary and general election campaign that further complicated matters. She stated,

> There was an ad that he sponsored and one that was a dark-money PAC ad paid for on his behalf. The other thing that factored into [the primary] and also in the general was these dark-money PACs. One reported to be on my behalf. And what happened there was that a particular PAC aired cheesy, crude, and tacky ads against my opponent. I started getting hate emails and phone calls and people on the doorsteps irate at me. They didn't understand that I had nothing to do with those ads, that under our state's ethics laws, I cannot have any type of communication with those individuals. They're independent expenditures, and I could be fined if I talk to them. I was very careful not to have any communication with these groups. But at the same time, it left me in a very defensive position. I denounced them and told everyone who would listen. I even spent five or six thousand dollars of my own money on a mailer to people in my district telling them that I didn't have anything to do with the [PACs]. And yet, people do not read the fine print that says the ad is not authorized or paid for by [the candidate]. (2020, Republican, Great Plains state, won primary, lost in general)

Political Parity's report *Right the Ratio* asserted that female Republican candidates have a more difficult time raising money, largely due to "fragmented sources of support."[20] Interestingly, after reviewing campaign-finance data from the Federal Election Commission, Political Parity found that, in general, male and female candidates receive very little money directly from the party, and PAC money is typically unavailable until a candidate becomes the actual party nominee. In review of this situation, the *Right the Ratio* report asserted, "This presents a paradox: without money, female GOP [Republican] candidates struggle to win their primaries, but they generally don't receive much party money until they do."[21]

Emily's List (Early Money Is Like Yeast), established in 1985, helps fund pro-choice Democrat female candidates, has raised over $600 million for candidates, has trained over nine thousand women, and boasts a community of over five million people.[22] Organizations that support Republican women include the Susan B. Anthony List, VIEW PAC, Maggie's List, and Winning For Women. None of these come close to matching the scale and scope of Emily's List, which distributes over $40 million per election cycle, compared to approximately $1.5 million spent by PACs supporting Republican female candidates. It is important to reiterate that the Democrat and Republican Parties have distinctly different cultures. The difference is also seen in the various ways the parties provide financial support for candidates. The Republican Party prioritizes party loyalty, whereas the Democratic Party responds more to group-based demands. For example, the Susan B. Anthony List will fund male candidates to defeat and decrease the number of Democrat women officeholders.[23]

Going forward, Republican Party leadership will need to better promote these organizations in order to close the influence gap that female Democrats currently enjoy through Democratic-leaning groups such as Emily's List. One avenue to achieve equity for Republican women would be for Republican state party leadership to take the lead in building bridges between Republican women and organizations that can then help support their campaigns and subsequently become valuable resources in the process.[24]

Campaigning Experiences: Fundraising,
Messaging, and Stereotyping

Once in full campaign mode, women are just as efficient and effective with campaign finances as men are.[25] There are, however, a few caveats with respect to fundraising that reflect ways women may see this all-important task differently than men do. One noteworthy distinction is that female candidates rely more heavily on female donors to finance their campaigns. For instance, in 2020, women donors gave nearly half (46 percent) of their contributions to women candidates while making up only 24 percent of contributions to male candidates.[26] Another factor is that women perceive fundraising to be harder for them than for men. A CAWP recruitment study reported that 56 percent of women believed fundraising was more difficult for women than for men. In contrast, 90 percent of men believed that fundraising was equally as hard for men as it was for women.[27] In this context, one respondent stated,

> Fundraising is particularly difficult for women running for state office [as] some organizations still give less to women then to men. (2018)

The necessity of fundraising is often front and center as one of the most critical pieces of a successful campaign. However, a second aspect of campaign finance involves the expense side of the ledger. In this instance, concerns have been raised over restrictive campaign spending laws that may make it more difficult for women to execute a campaign on par with their opponent. One example of a spending restriction has been not to allow child care as a legitimate campaign expense. As of 2020, nearly twenty states had approved some form of deduction for child care directly related to campaigning.[28] One respondent echoed this need and suggested that a few additional expenses be considered as permissible if the goal is to expand who runs and remove some of the hurdles associated with campaigning:

> There needs to be more discussion about how to support candidates besides traditional campaign expenditures, assisting with child care, household, food, car, etc., and making it easier especially for people who are not wealthy. (2020, Democrat)

In addition to the candidate's personal staff, party support and funding greatly impact a candidate's run for office. While state parties may be interested in expanding opportunities for female candidates, their decisions for distributing limited resources are centrally focused on keeping safe districts and flipping competitive districts into the party column. Other funding sources, such as Emily's List, can help bolster the prospects of women implementing more effective campaigns. At the same time, the more a candidate is tied directly to the state party, or to a PAC, the less control the individual campaign may have over the message. Overall party support reported by respondents was mixed. Republican respondents reported less support than Democrat respondents did.

We see a great deal of negative attacks that seem to dominate messaging in today's highly partisan environment. This approach may or may not be compatible with the way women choose to campaign. Krupnikov and Bauer found that female candidates are often disproportionately punished for instigating negative tactics.[29] Their research suggests that a female candidate may be considerably more constrained when it comes to campaign strategy. Women report an unwillingness to lie and engage in negative attacks even if doing so would increase their chances of winning.[30] Other research suggests that female candidates who focus on women's issues while simultaneously targeting social groups geared toward women fare better in achieving electoral success than other candidates do.[31] Additionally, there is some evidence that women employ a more collaborative leadership style over more power-wielding attributes associated with masculine leadership qualities.[32] One respondent illustrated many of these attributes, which in her view are preferable to the extreme negativity and attack-oriented politics of today. She explained,

> I think people were hungry for our message of listening and working together. We just ignored negative attacks. We didn't want to give oxygen to them. My professional background is in health care. I am an executive-level health-care professional. I have also served on community-level

boards. Experience and expertise matters. Another female candidate who is a nurse ran in a nearby district and lost by 1 percent. I think the difference there was she focused on social justice issues. I focused only on health care. (2020, Democrat, upper Midwest state, won)

Another respondent echoed the benefits of more women in state legislatures. She also wrapped the message in issues that were important to her and had fueled her motivation to run. She stated,

> I ran with the belief that we need more women in the halls of government. I believe that we bring a unique perspective that favors women, especially about children and families. I am also a strong advocate of women's issues and women having a seat at the table. I flipped a traditionally red seat after thirty-six years that many considered unflippable. I relished that challenge of running in a suburban district where voters tend to be more moderate and have more in common than what divides us ideologically. (2020)

One respondent emphasized the significance of running as a female Democrat. For her, presenting a message that resonated in the district was paramount. She stated,

> I believe that representation matters, so more women in government are necessary to reflect the issues important to the Democratic Party and the electorate in my district. (2020)

However, in other instances, clarity of message was not so simple to piece together. One Democrat respondent complained that the party's message was too nuanced and complex compared to Republicans:

> Democrats have struggled with messaging for a long time. The message from Democrats is too nuanced and complex. The Republicans have the same problem but overcome it with buzz words that don't really address

the issues. For example, Republicans aren't really pro-life but are only pro-birth. How do you message important issues in good faith in only one or two words? (2020, Democrat, upper Midwest state, lost)

Another Democrat respondent who lost echoed this view:

Republicans put forth simplistic authoritarian-type answers, whereas Democrats have multilayered, hard-to-process messages. [They need to] simplify messages. (2020, Democrat, Texas, lost)

Similarly, the following respondent was unable to break through the noise. In her view, the hostile political environment effectively muted her message. She stated,

The national scene was impeding my state house race. Most people were not paying attention at all about what was going on locally. The local issues I wanted to focus on were being drowned out by what's good or bad for the country. By the end of the election, [my opponent] had done such a good job of just hitting us with stuff 24/7. It was almost impossible to get any message across at all. (2020, Democrat, Missouri, lost)

In addition to the national message interfering with her campaign, this respondent also addressed how she stuck to a fact-based message, despite admitting that it was not likely to be as effective:

Conservatives do such a good job of just hitting you with stuff. It's almost impossible to be a candidate and get any message in at all. I sent out mailers with specific information on what I supported and pointed out specific bills my opponent voted for that impacted our district. So I give—which is a criticism of Democrats—a too detailed message, but I had to include the number of the bill so people could look it up as factual. (2020, Democrat, Missouri, lost)

The following respondent chose not to react to negative attacks, however, and chose to instead focus on issues and a fact-based message that turned out to be a winning campaign strategy. She stated,

> The Republican messaging against me was very socialist, and I am a moderate. I was endorsed by Biden, but the ads they put out had pictures associating me with Bernie and AOC. There were very dark images with burning buildings and riots. The ads were used against all Democrats in the state, not just me. We just ignored the attacks, deciding not to give oxygen to it. We did put out some fact-checking materials but stuck to our message of health care and that experience and expertise matters. I live in a highly educated district, and we tried to particularly connect with women voters. (2020, Democrat, Wisconsin, won)

One candidate who had previously ran unopposed in 2018 faced a challenger in 2020 who ran attack ads against her. To her surprise, she found that she needed to respond to those negative attacks and state her objections. She explained,

> During the first two times I ran, I had no crazy negative ads run against me. My first run, a special election was a fast [thirty-day] run, and I had interviews along with the other candidate but no negatives. Second run, I was unopposed. I could not believe how upsetting negative posts and ads on Facebook were during the current run. I could shrug it off, but it was upsetting because of the unfairness and inability to defend myself. (2020, Democrat, Iowa)

On balance, respondents reported being the recipients of negative attacks, not the instigators of attack tactics. In these instances, candidates resisted fighting back with negative attacks of their own and at times chose to ignore them. The examples offered here tend to mirror findings of previous research that female candidates may not be well served by engaging in negative partisan attacks. Instead, respondents tended to adopt a moderating and collaborative tone, with messaging that focused on issues particularly important to women voters, such as education and health care.

Stereotypes about the role of women in familial settings were reported by several respondents. The following comments were made to candidates by both male and female voters:

> "I can't vote for you. You're a woman." I had to remind the voter that both candidates in my district were female. (2020, Democrat, Ohio)

> "How does your husband feel about you running? Are you taking care of your household?" (2020, Democrat, Ohio)

> I recall voters asking, "Do you have kids?" Another voter assumed I had children and asked, "How old are your kids?" Questions I am not sure would be asked of a man. (2020, Democrat, Missouri)

Interestingly, one respondent noted that her worst critics were women, not men:

> I think that running as a woman has its unique challenges. After every public forum, a different woman would come up to me and offer constructive criticism. No one does that to a man. (2018)

It is quite common for campaigns to be heavily laced with partisan and negative attacks. For some respondents, it was difficult to determine if attack-style campaign tactics were crossing the line to gender-based attacks. One respondent commented on the negative attacks from her male opponent in this way, emphasizing that allegations of being incompetent and unprepared were more related to her being a female:

> The personal attacks on me were beyond the pale. Finally, people started calling me and said, "Okay, I was going to vote for the other guy, but I'm

not now." And people who knew me, supported me, and were going to vote for me anyway said, "What do you need? We're going to contribute again. We're going to volunteer." I even had some friends who were Democrats who said, "What can we do? We'll help because you shouldn't have to deal with this kind of demolishing of your character." It all was not only to attack; it was every aspect of my character. He tried to show me as incompetent and unprepared and lacking any integrity. It was just crazy. (2020, Republican, Great Plains state, urban, lost)

Another respondent noted several instances when men, in her view, were sexist toward her candidacy:

I think it exists out there, the sexism. There was a time at the polls two men approached me and harassed me. I had recently noticed where AOC had been harassed on the steps of the Capitol by a male congressman, and it really resonated with me. No woman has ever approached me and talked to me so hatefully. I thought it was that they were bigger than me and they could intimidate me. They treated me like I was this little lady standing there and they could scare me. The social order was always a certain way, and now people are trying to change things, and it scares some of the men out there. (2020, Democrat, Missouri, lost)

Gender-related comments were not always negative. For instance, one candidate noted that voters appreciated that a woman would bring a much-needed perspective to the state capital:

Voters would tell me it was important to keep a woman in the seat [the female incumbent had retired] and that having more women in the state legislature was important. I didn't experience any situations where my gender was a problem. (2020, Democrat, upper Midwest state, won)

Across two election cycles, 2018 and 2020, we found respondents to be fully cognizant that gender played a role in their campaigns. That said, they also strived to be seen simply as candidates. For the most part, they discussed that the way they campaigned was mostly a function of the political realities of the times.

COVID-19: An Unexpected Journey

It would be an understatement to say COVID-19 greatly impacted all of society, let alone campaigning, during 2020. No one could have predicted a pandemic becoming a significant intervening variable in how campaigns were conducted. Obviously, the pandemic made the 2020 election an outlier, far from the norm of the traditional campaign model.[33] While this unfortunate situation applied to everyone running for office, we could not have accurately assessed the experiences of women running for office without considering how COVID impacted their lives.[34] Thus, we included questions in our survey related to campaigning during COVID.

One respondent, a rebound candidate, noted the differences in campaigning in 2018 and 2020 and contrasted the benefits and drawbacks of campaigning from home, balancing home-life responsibilities with work, and relying more extensively on social media:

> Obviously we have to consider our families. My husband was supportive, and that makes a difference. In 2018, I hated missing out on dinners with my kids while I was canvassing, but due to COVID, I got to have dinner with them every night in 2020. A woman who is a mom has to consider her children. I made time to help my older boys with their college applications, for example. (2020, rebound candidate)

As for first-time female candidates, one respondent was looking forward to the challenge of learning and checking off all the boxes associated with campaigning. Disappointment ensued when the face-to-face aspects of campaigning were put on hold. She shared,

National politics—voters who don't always vote came out in droves to support the Trump train—many straight-ticket voters. COVID prevented me
from connecting with voters in person, which might have been the anti-
dote to Trump on the down-ticket races. (2020, Democrat, Kentucky, lost)

Democrat respondents noted that the failure of Republican candidates to follow Centers for Disease Control (CDC) guidelines hurt their
efforts to adequately message and subsequently get out the vote. One
respondent commented,

> National politics and high voter turnout to support Trump, state politics
> & high level of support for Republican Gov. Inability to connect directly
> with voters due to COVID 19. (2020, Democrat, New Hampshire, lost)

A few Democrat candidates tried to do some traditional campaigning,
wearing masks and staying six feet apart, and reported mixed results.
One candidate expressed frustration with her Republican opponent,
who refused to make any adjustments to her campaign, and with the
Democratic Party for putting in place rules that required candidates to
operate virtual campaigns:

> I am a Democrat in a R district, but I won by six points. National politics
> and an inability to canvass likely made my margin less than it would have
> been otherwise. (2020, Democrat, southern state, won)

For another Democrat candidate following CDC guidelines was the right
thing to do but put the campaign at a clear disadvantage. She stated,

> My opponent completely ignored COVID restrictions, held public gath-
> erings, no masks, no social distancing, and door knocking—far more ef-
> fective than relying on mailers and phone calls. (2020, Democrat, New
> Hampshire, lost)

One Republican implied that the outcome of her race might have improved if she were able to physically campaign as usual to counter the anti-Trump messaging dominating the campaign:

> I believe that the negative media every day for our president played a negative role. COVID made it harder to actually knock on people's doors and speak to them face-to-face. (2020, Republican, New Mexico, lost)

For one Democrat respondent, the COVID campaign experience revealed important insights about how campaigns might look in the future following a pandemic. She shared,

> I felt showing up at the door with a mask was very disrespectful. We relied on phone banks and primarily text messages rather than direct phone calls. Texting was more effective. People wouldn't answer phone calls but would respond to texts. We were more technology oriented, using Facebook, Twitter, Instagram, and social media ads. (2020, Democrat, Minnesota, won)

Going forward, candidates and campaign researchers ought to more closely scrutinize the strategies and tactics candidates used when they campaigned during COVID. Among our findings, candidates became more acutely aware of the uses and misuses of social media in order to adjust to campaigning during a pandemic. Accordingly, candidates paid close attention to when and how to incorporate Facebook, Twitter, and Instagram into their campaigns. Respondents conveyed frustration over COVID but adjusted their campaigns accordingly. The pandemic was not going to derail the decision they made to run.

Conclusion

In this chapter, we have explored how a complex web of factors intersected with the campaigns of women running for the state legislature during the Trump era. A great deal of research exists on whether women campaign differently from men. The consensus is that men and women generally do not campaign differently.[35] Consistent with the literature, respondents conveyed a mastery of the things that any candidate needs to do in order to compete for a seat. By the same token, respondents provided examples of political campaign experiences that were unique to female candidates.

At the micro level, respondents commented on important elements of campaigning, including campaign training programs, party relations, messaging, and the influence of PACs. Respondents conveyed skill in the execution of campaign activities while tackling gender-related challenges on the campaign trail. These obstacles ranged from voters questioning why they were running to the party's (in particular, the Republican Party's) failure to address the gender equity gap in state legislatures. Their campaigns also had to function in a politically charged climate of hyperpartisanship, personified by the Trump effect. This was especially challenging for women running as Democrats, many of whom were motivated to run in reaction to the highly charged views espoused by Donald Trump, only to find that pro-Trump and anti-Trump attitudes were just as strong in state legislative politics. Our understanding of gender and politics can benefit from a more contextual examination of the decisions women make on the campaign trail.[36] We have sought to add to the literature by tracing the campaign experiences of state legislative candidates across two election cycles. Overall, respondents presented themselves as enthusiastic and skilled campaigners able to tackle foreseeable and unexpected challenges, such as a pandemic within a chaotic political environment.

5

The Urban-Rural Divide

Opportunities and Obstacles

Despite what the pundits want us to think, contested primaries aren't civil war; they are democracy at work, and that's
beautiful.
—Sarah Palin, former governor of Alaska and vice presidential candidate

A contemporary book about women and politics would not be complete
without a discussion regarding the urban-rural divide that currently
exists in partisan politics. Most media coverage of the national political
climate is focused on what occurs in Washington, DC. In reality, political differences in society are played out at the state and local level across
the nation.[1] Researchers have observed a growing urban-rural divide as
further evidence of the deep divisions that are permeating US society.[2]
The geography of the United States is largely composed of rural counties
that overwhelmingly vote for Republicans. In contrast, Democrats are
concentrated in counties with dense urban populations of one hundred
thousand or greater.[3]

A stark contrast also exists in the economic growth and development patterns between urban and rural counties. Urban counties
account for 70 percent of gross domestic product (GDP), and rural
counties account for 29 percent.[4] Socioeconomic status and urban
density also contribute to urban Democratic strongholds.[5] A recent
report by CityLab sought to identify the spectrum of the urban-rural
divide by categorizing states by how friendly state legislatures are toward urban growth and development as opposed to rural interests.

On the political spectrum, Gimpel et al. found that the geographic distance between small towns and major central cities, combined with population density, was a strong indicator of party affiliation.[6] Their research provided further evidence that those who share the same geographic space tend to share similar political beliefs. This idea is captured by Leatherby, who writes, "This is more than just an ideological gap. The physical landscape both groups inhabit have become so different that it is easy for urbanites and rural Americans to lose touch with how those in other parts of the country feel."[7] Another study found that states with pro-urban legislatures were far outpacing anti-urban states with regard to forward-looking economic development. Pro-urban economic growth states were more likely to be controlled by Democrats, and anti-urban states were more likely to be controlled by Republicans.[8] Fiorina perhaps best sums up this phenomenon: "But when Democrats are largely an urban party and Republicans a suburban and rural party, why should anyone expect Republican representatives to worry about the problems of the cities? Conversely, why should Democrats worry about the economic consequences of environmental laws for farmers and ranchers? Urbanites vote for Democrats and rural farm regions vote for Republicans. Party homogeneity encourages both parties to reject trade-offs and advocate one-sided programs that reflect the parties' preponderant interests."[9]

To provide a feel for what this geographic gap looks like, we need to look no further than the results of the 2020 presidential election, in which Joe Biden won 477 urban and suburban counties, compared to the 2,497 predominantly rural counties won by President Trump.[10] The difference in the outcome in 2020 compared to 2016 was Biden's ability to perform five percentage points better than Hillary Clinton in suburban counties, while rural and urban areas remained overwhelmingly partisan.[11] Since 2008, the urban-rural partisan gap has widened in presidential elections, putting an even greater premium on winning in the suburbs as illustrated in figure 5.1.[12]

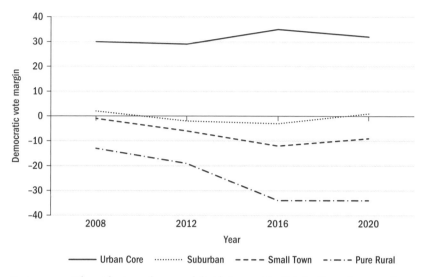

FIGURE 5.1. The widening urban-rural divide in presidential elections: Democratic vote margins, 2008–2021 (Frey, 2020)

In this chapter, we examine how women legislative candidates in our study ran in the 2018 and 2020 election cycles from a political geography perspective. Our intent is to create a clearer picture of the political landscape facing candidates and how the urban-rural divide will continue to shape relationships between female candidates and voters across state legislative districts. This information could be valuable for any candidate running for the state legislature, but our focus on women candidates reveals specific takeaways relevant for this demographic group for several reasons. First, we can better understand the ways women seek to match their personal motivations for running with the political realities of their district. This information could be especially important for better understanding what motivates first-time candidates to run and what experiences better equip rebound candidates to run again. Second, by exploring ways women campaign within the urban-rural continuum, we may gain a greater appreciation for how they campaigned and what they learned about politics and voters in their district. For candidates contemplating running for a state legislative seat, this insight about what other candidates experienced in the 2018 and 2020 election cycles, in light of their district and the political geographic landscape in which it is situated, could be helpful to their decision-making journey and their campaign.

A study by Montgomery focused on the urban-rural divide in the politically competitive state of Minnesota.[13] While Minnesota has trended toward Democrats, the Republican Party has made significant progress in rural areas of the state. The significant uptick of Republican support in rural Minnesota, according to Montgomery, was tied to the Trump effect, as shown in figure 5.2.

For our research, we adopted the CityLab Congressional Density Index (CDI), which classifies urban-rural areas to analyze congressional and state legislature elections.[14] The categories identified by Florida and Montgomery in CityLab's CDI are geographic indicators that classify the 435 congressional districts in the US on a continuum from urban to rural.[15] The six geographic classifications and descriptions and the number of congressional districts in each category are highlighted in

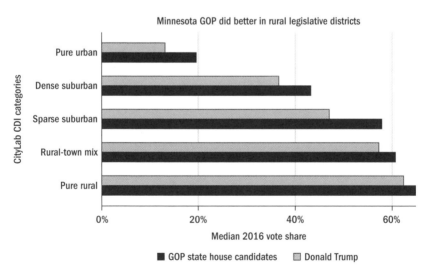

FIGURE 5.2. Comparing support for Republican candidates with support for President Trump in Minnesota (Bloomberg CityLab; Montgomery, 2018)

table 5.1, along with the corresponding voter percentage for the presidential candidates in 2016 and 2020. It is important to understand the geographic context and how it shaped these two election cycles. A quick glance at table 5.1 will help to understand why geography, specifically suburban districts, have become so important to state races.

The CityLab model generally captures the literature on the relationship between geography and politics in the current political environment. We incorporated the CityLab model into our research to ascertain a clearer picture of the political geography of the districts in which our respondents were running. We asked survey respondents in which state legislative district they were running as well as the federal congressional district that the legislative district was embedded within. In many cases, state legislative districts capture more than one congressional district. We also asked respondents to identify on a sliding scale from 1 (urban) to 100 (rural) where they would classify their district. While this is a subjective way to capture the geography of the districts, it gave us a way to measure our respondents' subjective perception. During interviews with the twenty-three respondents with whom we conducted an in-depth interview, we asked them to describe their district. After doing so, we determined that we should use both this subjective measure of geographic district and CityLab's CDI. Using respondents' information about their congressional district, we classified the districts into the six CityLab CDI categories identified by Florida and Montgomery.[16]

In table 5.2, we provide percentages of 2020 survey respondents in each category, based on their identified congressional district. We also used the sliding urban-to-rural (1–100) scale from our 2018 and 2020 surveys to capture the perspective of the respondents. We found that the CDI classification was not always consistent with how respondents described their district. Therefore, we modified the CityLab CDI. We discuss this in more detail later in this chapter. We also include how we coded the sliding scale in table 5.2, so that you can visualize how it would compare to the CityLab CDI categories. We ran a correlation to measure for consistency using respondents' congressional district as

TABLE 5.1. Breakdown of Support for Presidential Candidates in 2016 and 2020 by CityLab CDI Geographic Category

Classification	Description	Number of districts (% of total 435 congressional districts)	Trump voters in 2016 (%)	Trump voters in 2020 (%)	Clinton voters in 2016 (%)	Biden voters in 2020 (%)
Pure rural	Mix of very rural areas and some small cities with some suburban-style areas	70 (16)	62	62	34	36%
Rural-suburban mix	Significant suburban and rural populations with almost no dense urban neighborhoods	114 (26)	57	57	38	41
Sparse suburban	Predominantly suburban, with a mix of sprawling exurb-style or denser neighborhoods (inner-ring suburbs); may contain small rural populations and a small urban core	86 (20)	47	46	48	52
Dense suburban	Predominantly suburban, especially denser inner-ring suburbs; also a significant urban population	83 (19)	38	38	56	60
Urban-suburban mix	Mix of urban areas and inner-ring suburbs	48 (11)	29	32	66	67
Pure urban	Dense urban neighborhoods	34 (8)	18	22	79	77

Source: Florida and Montgomery, 2018; Nir, 2020.

TABLE 5.2. Percentage of Survey Respondents by CityLab CDI Geographic Category

Classification	Description	% in our 2020 study, based on respondent congressional district	Categories from survey (urban-rural continuum slider scale value range)	% in our 2020 study, based on response to slider scale (N = 219)	% in our 2018 study, based on response to slider scale (N = 569)
Pure rural	Mix of very rural areas and some small cities with some suburban-style areas	21 (*n* = 47)	Rural (80–100)	21 (*n* = 46)	26 (*n* = 148)
Rural-suburban mix	Significant suburban and rural populations with almost no dense urban neighborhoods	31 (*n* = 68)	Rural-suburban mix (60–79)	22 (*n* = 49)	24 (*n* = 137)
Sparse suburban	Predominantly suburban, with a mix of sprawling exurb-style or denser neighborhoods (inner-ring suburbs); may contain small rural populations and a small urban core	27 (*n* = 60)	Sparse suburban and dense suburban (40–59)	36 (*n* = 80)	28 (*n* = 161)
Dense suburban	Predominantly suburban, especially denser inner-ring suburbs; also a significant urban population	*13 (n = 28)*			
Urban-suburban mix	Mix of urban areas and inner-ring suburbs	5 (*n* = 12)	Urban-suburban mix (20–39)	11 (*n* = 24)	12 (*n* = 69)
Pure urban	Dense urban neighborhoods	1 (*n* = 3)	Urban (0–19)	9 (*n* = 20)	9 (*n* = 54)

Source: CityLab, 2018.

categorized by the CityLab CDI and the value that respondents reported in our survey using the sliding-scale continuum that best described their district. The results indicate a consistency between the two geographic measures (rs = .429, p = .000).

Geography and Running for State Legislature

In recent election cycles, the importance of geography has become clear. The respondents in our research conveyed the importance of geography in both the 2018 midterm and the 2020 general elections. Using our five categories (modified from the CityLab CDI), we looked at the association between political party and whether the candidate won or lost her race. Table 5.3 summarizes these chi-square associations and results.

TABLE 5.3. Campaign Outcomes by Candidate, Political Party, and Geographic Category in 2018 and 2020

2018 (N = 228)

	Pure rural		Rural-suburban mix*		Sparse/dense suburban		Urban-suburban mix**		Pure urban***	
	Won	Lost	Won	Lost	Won	Lost	Won	Lost	Won	Lost
Republican	3	2	8	0	7	8	1	2	1	2
Democrat	9	44	7	28	23	31	18	5	13	1

χ^2 = * 19.1, p = .000
χ^2 = ** 8.73, p = .033
χ^2 = *** 13.82, p = .001

2020 (N = 214)

	Pure rural+		Rural-suburban mix++		Sparse/dense suburban		Urban-suburban mix+++		Pure urban++++	
	Won	Lost	Won	Lost	Won	Lost	Won	Lost	Won	Lost
Republican	13	2	9	1	8	13	1	4	0	7
Democrat	3	31	4	34	32	25	13	5	9	3

χ^2 = + 24.3, p = .000
χ^2 = ++ 25.32, p = .000
χ^2 = +++ 4.48, p = .034
χ^2 = ++++ 9.98, p = .002

For 2018 respondents, there was a significant association between those who won their race and whether they were Republican or Democrat in urban, urban-suburban mix, and rural-suburban mix categories. In these three categories, we found that Democrats were winning in more urban geographic areas and Republicans were more likely to win in rural areas. Interestingly, there was no significant association in the sparse/dense suburban category when it came to political party and whether a respondent won or lost her race. This indicates that both Republicans and Democrats were just as likely to win in those areas as they were to lose.

For 2020 respondents, there was a significant association between those who won their race and whether they were Republican or Democrat in every geographic category except the sparse/dense suburban category. As partisan politics would predict, more Democrats than Republicans were winning in more urban or dense geographic areas, and more Republicans than Democrats were winning in more rural or less dense geographic areas. The lack of a significant association in the suburban areas again indicates that both Republicans and Democrats can win (or lose) in those areas, so the suburbs are anyone's game.

In addition to table 5.3, which simply illustrates the importance of the suburbs for both Republican and Democrat candidates, it is important to more fully capture illustrations of campaign environments based on the five geographic categories. The intent here is to add flavor to what campaigning looked like for state legislative candidates from our research across the political geography of the US. These examples show that female candidates were adept at presenting a campaign that spoke to the demographics of their district. In order to highlight the political geography of each category, we gathered specific campaign information from ballotpedia.org, statisticalatlas.com, ivoterguide .com, ourcampaigns.com, and votesmart.org. We accessed websites, Facebook, Twitter, and Instagram pages of specific respondents from our research, along with their opponents, to better understand their campaigns.

On the basis of the information provided by respondents in the 2020 survey, we took a deeper dive into the nature of the campaigns of female candidates across each of the five (modified) geographic categories. Our intent is not to put a spotlight on any specific respondent or candidate but rather to convey how candidates shaped their campaigns to reflect the political geography of their district. By highlighting some of the campaigns from these specific geographic areas, we shed light on the continued importance of the suburbs in recent election cycles and how state legislative races will be impacted by the suburbs in future election cycles. For it is in the suburbs where we see the most competitive races and the most opportunities for both Democrat and Republican women to run for and win state legislative seats. Rural areas continue to be out of reach for most Democrat candidates, and urban areas remain off-limits to Republican candidates.

These political geographic divisions suggest that women interested in running for state legislative seats must address both commonly reported gender-based barriers to running and also a political landscape that narrows the playbook for them as candidates. Being more intentional about recruiting women whose beliefs align with the political geography of a district could assist with increasing the number of women who run and win elections. Conversely, not recognizing the reality of the urban-rural divide could work against increasing the number of female state legislators. The following examples from the five geographic categories reveal that it is important for female candidates to be a good "fit" for their district.

Running in Rural America: Pure Rural Districts

Among respondents from areas categorized as pure rural, as expected, Democrat female candidates struggled to compete for seats. Of the forty-four Democrat respondents running in pure rural areas, only three were elected in these districts. In one instance, a female Democrat candidate was aided by the fact that she was running in a multirepresentative district, earning a seat to the state legislature by finishing second to her Republican opponent. Absent a multiple representation formula, it is unlikely that she would have been elected in a rural state where the Republican Party holds 90 percent of the state legislative seats. The Democrat respondent described her multirepresentative race this way:

> I got the second most votes, and the top two were elected. I would have liked to get more Republicans to vote for me, but not sure how I would have accomplished that. (2020)

The other two Democrat respondents who won in rural areas emerged from running in districts with small urban pockets that dot vast rural and otherwise solid-red states. For instance, one female Democrat benefited from running in a district with a small city of around thirty thousand people that is the home of an institution of higher education.[17] Another female respondent won in a rural region where there was a long history of voting for Democrat candidates. Her district had become more purple over the past several decades and is surrounded by rural districts that have dramatically flipped from blue to red as the urban-rural divide has grown throughout her home state. The respondent was able to win a closely contested election in a rural district due to the vote from an urban pocket within the district. Two other Democrat respondents who won in rural areas serve in states where the Republican Party holds the trifecta of control of both legislative chambers and the governor's office. Additionally, the three Democrat winners became members of Democratic Party caucuses that make up less than 5 percent of the legislative body in each of the three state legislatures in which they serve.

The overwhelming reality for Democrats who ran in rural areas was that they were destined for defeat. The following respondents all lost their bids, by large margins. One female Democrat respondent spoke to the lack of party support for her campaign due to the red and more rural district in which she ran:

> I am in a traditionally red district. The Democratic Party has been almost no help. When I see party endorsements or funding that targets competitive districts and they don't say anything else about the rest of us, it just makes it even harder to do the hard work of running a serious campaign. I have had party officials tell me to my face, . . . "You know you can't win, right?" While I know the hardcore realities of statistics, I don't have to be reminded of it from the party. (2018)

Similarly, another female Democrat candidate decried the failure of the Democratic Party to find a pathway to reach rural voters:

> The Democratic Party needs to take a serious look at how it runs campaigns in rural areas of the nation if it wants to take back the traditional rural family farmers and working poor. It also needs to do some soul searching about how to build a bench in red states and red districts. The Democratic Party is never going to regain the ground they have lost in red rural counties if they continue to abandon us and only target candidates in the clusters of liberal dwellers in the more urban areas in the red states. (2018)

Among Republican respondents, only two lost in pure rural areas. In one instance, the Republican candidate was running in a multirepresentative district and lost to another female Republican candidate who finished first and a female Democrat who finished second. The second female Republican respondent, who ran in a pure rural district, lost in a very close race to a Democrat incumbent by less than 1 percent of the vote. The Republican respondent's district also included a small Democrat-leaning urban pocket. In the few rural districts that were more competitive, the urban areas were small cities between twenty and forty thousand residents.[18]

Running in Rural-Suburban Mix Districts

A rural-suburban area is defined as having significant suburban and rural populations with almost no dense urban neighborhoods.[19] In these areas, nine of ten Republican respondents secured state legislative seats. Meanwhile, only 37 percent of female Democrat respondents won in rural-suburban districts. Examples of what a typical campaign looked like for women running for the state legislature in rural-suburban districts follow.

A Democrat respondent lost in a district just outside a major metropolitan area in a Pacific Coast state and described her experience this way:

> Our district is controlled by local party influences. It's hard to break through that. (2020)

She lost by a ten-point margin to a Republican male incumbent. In her campaign, she emphasized women's health, climate change, and the cost of living.[20] Her opponent ranks as a moderate conservative.[21] The district had voted for a Democrat as recently as 2012.[22] Another female Democrat respondent lost a rural-suburban district race to a very conservative male opponent. Her campaign message emphasized her support of education, her trust in facts, and her support for the Second Amendment.[23] Her opponent offered a conservative pro-life and pro-gun message.[24] She lost by twenty-three percentage points. Another rural-suburban Democrat respondent described how her race looked:

> There was an unprecedented turnout in the rural parts of my district, likely activated by the presidential race. There was an absolute torrent of early negative, slanderous ads and mailers for weeks, well before I could define myself. That was part of a national and state strategy against Democrats. There was an unprecedented amount of money spent in the district because it was seen as competitive. (2020)

On the other hand, one Democrat respondent won by a ten-point margin in a rural-suburban district in a southeastern state. Her district includes a sliver of a more metropolitan urban area but otherwise has a significant rural geography.[25]

A closer examination of a rural suburban district in which a Republican respondent won revealed three small cities with between 20,000 and 30,000 residents. The three communities are roughly fifteen to thirty miles apart, with the remainder of the district rural and a spattering of small towns of around 1,000 people. With a total population of around 120,000 residents, the three small cities make up nearly 70 percent of the district. This respondent described her rural-suburban district this way:

> Fifty percent urban and fifty percent rural, and there are major urban centers thirty to forty-five minutes away, that are outside the district. (2020)

The district has economic ties to the larger urban centers outside the district and thus has somewhat of a suburban feel inside its boundaries.[26] This Republican candidate viewed the voters within the district as more centrist and not prone to embrace negative or divisive politics, saying in her interview,

> I had worked on many local campaigns and have been civically engaged most of my adult life, including serving on boards. I thought I was done, but the incumbent retired, so [for me] the time was right. I emphasized my experience and a positive message throughout the campaign. My opponent, also a first-time candidate, played to anger to the point where I had Democrats supporting me. (2020)

Her Democrat opponent in the race, a first-time female candidate, ran on a message of improving education and health care. The Democrat's campaign message emphasized her moderate views to try to appeal to a broader spectrum of voters. Nevertheless, the female Republican respondent won by thirty percentage points.[27]

Overall, respondents reported that rural-suburban districts were slightly more competitive than rural districts. As expected, these districts still favored Republican candidates. Democrats fared somewhat better as population density increased. Nevertheless, suburban environments that were further removed from urban cores were more favorable for Republican respondents.

Running in Sparse Suburban / Dense Suburban Districts (the Suburbs)

The largest group of respondents in the survey classified their districts as sparse suburban / dense suburban ($n = 79$), as illustrated in figure 5.3—in other words, the suburbs. In addition, the sparse/dense suburban category produced the most competitive districts among the five political geographic categories. Competitive districts were those where respondents reported their electoral margin to be ±3 percent. In our research, 21 percent of female Democrat respondents reported running in competitive seats, compared to 9 percent of female Republican respondents. Ten Democrat respondents won and six lost in competitive sparse/dense suburban districts. Among female Republican respondents running in competitive sparse/dense suburban districts, two respondents won and four lost their elections.

We explored the ideological slant of respondents who ran in sparse suburban, suburban, and dense suburban districts. In particular, we were interested to see if we could find any evidence of candidates, in both parties, running more centrist campaigns in highly competitive districts where every vote counts. Our survey results reveal that extreme political ideology was not as evident in the campaigns of respondents who ran in competitive sparse/dense suburban districts. Of the ten Democrats who won, seven of the ten identified themselves as liberal or very liberal. One Democrat respondent who won identified as a centrist, and one identified as slightly conservative.

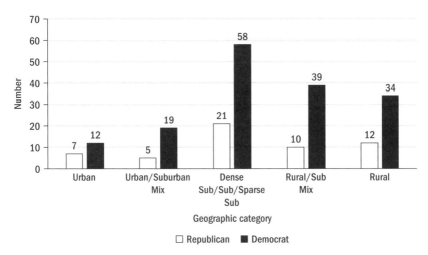

FIGURE 5.3. Number of Republicans and Democrats from 2020 survey by geographic category: suburbs (*N* = 217)

The number of Republican respondents who ran in competitive districts was even smaller, and all identified themselves as either conservative (*n* = 3; two won, one lost) or very conservative (*n* = 1; lost). A closer examination of how respondents campaigned in this suburban environment reveals that respondents of both parties were presenting predominantly moderate messages to voters in the most competitive races. At the same time, respondents were reporting negative attacks by their opponents and by PACs that sought to bind them to a liberal or conservative label.

One centrist approach to try and appeal to the sparse/dense suburban voter was revealed by a Democrat first-time candidate:

> I ran because of the pandemic. I am a health-care professional, and we are not managing the pandemic. I am a moderate, and experience and expertise matters. I live in a highly educated suburban district and saw movement [toward me] particularly with women voters in the district. We just ignored the attack ads and focused on our positive message. (2020, won)

The comments provided by this respondent need to be understood in the context of her opponent, an incumbent conservative Republican. In previous campaigns, he highlighted his pro-life, pro-gun, and low-taxes positions. He managed to win this competitive seat in 2018. However, this successful, first-time female candidate squeaked out a victory by a margin of less than 1 percent of the vote.[28]

A Republican respondent described in detail what it was like to run as a Republican in a dense suburban setting in what otherwise is a predominantly red state:

> President Trump came [here], and a lot of local Republican officials did not really want him to come because they feared rioting and protests. But it was held anyway. I wore my favorite "[my name] for legislature" T-shirt so I could be seen behind the stage as the president spoke and was on television as a result. And so I had a lot of people either hate that or love that about me. So my opponent used photos of me at the rally to show people that I was a Trump supporter, and that played into it enormously. The demographics in my district had changed. As I was door knocking, a lot of people on the doorsteps who were on my list, who were supposedly Republicans, were not Trump supporters. They said, "I've been a Republican for a long time, but I do not like President Trump." Trump barely won my district in 2016. And interestingly enough, our governor, who is a Republican, who won in 2018, didn't win this district. Polling showed me ten to twelve points down at the start of the campaign. So I had to make up all of that to be able to win, and I almost did. (2020, lost)

This quote illustrates the types of campaign we were seeing throughout the US suburbs. Respondents commonly campaigned, regardless of party affiliation, as voices of moderation and reason. At the same time, they faced mounting pressure from opponents who sought to paint them as too extreme.

Running in Urban-Suburban Mix Districts

As state legislative races move toward more densely populated areas, respondents in our survey reported being involved in few competitive races. The closest results were found in two multirepresentative districts. In one case, a female Democrat secured a seat by finishing in third place among six candidates. A majority of the candidates were females, and the winners received between 18 percent and 20 percent of the votes cast. In the other multirepresentative district, the Democrat respondent failed to secure a seat, finishing behind four Republican male candidates. The difference between being elected and falling short of earning a seat was a mere 1.5 percent. However, the other twenty-two female respondents who fell in the urban-suburban mix category were not involved in competitive races. The closest winning margins were between 5 and 7 percent. Upon closer examination of the remaining twenty-one races, survey respondents experienced noncompetitive races in which they were winning by margins ranging from ten to thirty points. In all but one instance, respondents who won ran as Democrats. Of the urban suburban respondents, 40 percent ran against at least one other female opponent.

Interestingly, all four of the Republican respondents from urban-suburban mix areas lost to a female Democrat opponent. Of the female Democrat respondents, 61 percent reported their political ideology as liberal or very liberal, with the remainder describing themselves as moderates. Two female Republican respondents labeled themselves as conservatives, with one of the two winning their election. The other three female Republican respondents described themselves as moderates. One Republican respondent emphasized fiscal responsibility and stayed away from controversial social issues, although she lost. She provided this perspective on running in her urban-suburban mix district:

> My district is currently not represented by anyone who is financially conservative, and I felt my voice was especially needed in the statehouse. I

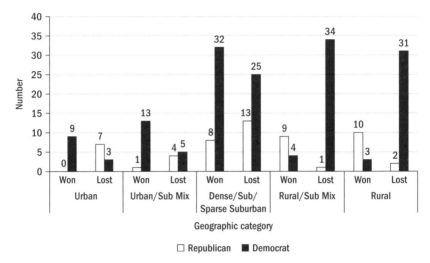

FIGURE 5.4. Number of Republicans and Democrats from 2020 survey by geographic category, mixed ($N = 214$)

didn't care about social issues or what you do in your bedroom. Trump was very controversial, and that factored into it. What the city, state, and federal government controls are not necessarily distinguishable to voters. (Republican, 2020, lost)

Another female Republican running in an urban-suburban mix district commented,

The voters in my district are mostly Democrats. Maybe they shouldn't be. They are pro-life and pro-freedom. But they have been told that Republicans are against them, and they tend to believe without doing any research. (2020, lost)

The takeaway from urban-suburban mix respondents is that female Democrat candidates presented themselves as further to the left than was typically the case in suburban districts and were overall successful in presenting voters with a liberal message. Republican respondents tried to connect with voters by presenting a more moderate message but were easily defeated. There was one exception of a female conservative Republican who ran and won in an urban-suburban mix district located in a predominantly Republican state.

Running in Pure Urban Districts

Only twenty respondents ran in districts that were categorized as pure urban. Nine female Democrat respondents reported that they won, while three others lost. There were only seven female Republican respondents who ran in pure urban districts, all of whom lost, although two were in competitive races. One Republican respondent running in a pure urban district simply stated, "The GOP has abandoned the urban core."

One of the Democrat respondents who lost blamed her defeat on gerrymandering. Another female Democrat lost to a female Republican from a major metropolitan area in a district composed of upper-socioeconomic-status neighborhoods. The remaining respondents who fit the pure urban category won with between 60 and 100 percent of the vote.[29] Over half of the respondents ran unopposed. In four instances, respondents identified their districts as competitive because of the primaries that they had to win in order to go through the formality of securing their seat in the November general election. One respondent described this one-party urban environment:

> The primary race was competitive, starting with four candidates, then in the end three. The primary was the big show, so getting my message out to constituents was instrumental. I also had to put in the work, often phone banking six to ten hours per day. That was huge too. The lack of door-to-door campaigning [due to COVID] made for a reliance on mailers and phone banking essential. (2020, won)

Winning candidates in these competitive Democratic Party primaries typically faced three to six opponents. Their winning margins were small, in the range of one to three percentage points, and their vote shares were between 25 and 35 percent, depending on the size of the primary field.[30]

Conclusion

What might the urban-rural divide tell us about the prospects of recruiting more female candidates? As previously discussed, geopolitical divisions may limit opportunities to expand the pool of candidates beyond the established partisan lean in which one resides. At least in the immediate future, more Republican women will need to run in rural areas, as female Democrat candidates continue to run in urban areas. The path forward for Republicans is murkier. Elder goes so far as to suggest that Republican women interested in running for a state legislative seat would be better off moving out of solid-red regions.[31] The stronger the Republican Party is in a state, the harder it is for Republican women to be supported to run and win seats.[32] One female Republican respondent may have summed up the problem in a nutshell when she said,

> Are there any other Eisenhower Republicans out there? This is getting lonely. (2018)

Dittmar examined Republican women who recently ran for Congress and reveals that many candidates tried to break the red-state political glass ceiling by presenting themselves as more masculine, aggressive, and relentless "fighters" to try to be a better "fit" for red-state voters.[33] Yet, according to Dittmar, too many female Republicans are running in noncompetitive primaries and general election districts where the odds of winning are stacked against them. It would seem that there are opportunities for conservative women from rural areas to run for the state legislature if a balance can be struck between ideology and gender identity.

The suburbs are currently the only region where expanding the pool of women candidates from both parties seems likely. In the suburbs, we could continue to see more general election races where women are running against women. As the suburbs have become the swing areas, it would seem that candidates from both parties would benefit electorally from promoting a more moderate or centrist message. The point here is that, although the goal of expanding the number of women running for state legislature is commendable, the slight incremental growth rate of women serving in state legislatures may continue well into the future, in part due to the urban-rural divide.

This is not to say that a person should not run in a district where one party or ideological slant is dominant. We noted several respondents who realized that they had no chance of winning but stated that they were proud of their effort and thought it was important for an alternative voice to be heard in their district. However, running candidates in nonwinnable seats will not achieve gender balance in state legislatures. The urban-rural divide has been a significant factor in US politics for decades.[34] In this environment, negative partisanship may be the best indicator of how a Democrat or a Republican will vote.[35] The unwillingness of voters to consider voting for the other side is readily apparent in the urban-rural divide. At present, there are no indications that negative partisanship will end anytime soon.[36] As one Democrat respondent who ran in a rural area commented,

> The current disdain for any Democrat definitely impacted the outcome. I live in a very Republican area, where many wouldn't look at anything other than the R or D behind their name. (2020)

The responsibility for expanding the number of female state legislators lies squarely on the leadership of both political parties. There are several short-term goals that should be considered. The Democratic

Party should continue to focus on recruiting more women to run in urban and suburban districts. Greater financial support for progressive female candidates to run in competitive primaries in urban and suburban areas is also a must. The Republican Party needs to explore ways to expand the number of women running for the state legislature in rural areas. A key consideration for female Republican candidates will be what type of message they need to adopt in order to run and win in very red districts while at the same time expanding their presence in the suburbs, where the political views of voters tend to be more moderate. Presently, the Republican Party discounts identity politics in its recruitment effort. Addressing this reality is just as important for Republican women to weigh as they contemplate running for office as it is for Republican Party leadership to wrestle with. Both parties need to closely examine how expanding the number of women in the state legislature will advance their policy goals in the highly partisan (urban-rural divide) world that both Democrats and Republicans have created.

The lesson here for women considering a run for a state legislative seat is to know your district. An important aspect of knowing the district is recognizing its political geography. In the process, a candidate may develop a clearer sense of how to connect with voters in her district. Developing a message that reflects political geography could go a long way toward addressing concerns raised by respondents in chapter 4 regarding the disconnect they observed between candidates, the party, and the voter. Of course, applying this "know your district" angle to the decision to run may limit who ultimately runs for the state legislature regardless of whether they are men or women.

The urban-rural divide suggests that only individuals with values that fit the district are likely to step forward as candidates and be supported by the party, donors, and voters. We found that the female respondents who won were a good fit for the political geography of their district. Conservatives fared better in rural areas, and liberals did quite well in urban areas. Respondents from suburban districts self-reported being more conservative or liberal rather than moderate. Most respondents reported trying to convey a more centrist message without abandoning what it means to be a Democrat or a Republican. The centrist strategy worked best for respondents of both parties who ran in the suburbs.

6

Expanding the Ranks

Where Do We Go from Here?

One of the lessons that I grew up with was to always stay
true to yourself and never let what somebody else says dis-
tract you from your goals.
—Michelle Obama, former First Lady

In hindsight, the Trump effect can be seen as an accelerant fueling
greater anger for those who increasingly felt alienated by decades of
leftward social change.[1] There is every indication that this clash of values will continue to infiltrate state and local politics. Early on in this
book, we referenced Tip O'Neill, who claimed, in the 1980s, that all politics is local.[2] Trump-era politics seem to have now become immersed
in state and local politics. In this political landscape, the Trump-era
"issue bucket" remains full and continues to drive state and local party
platforms and governing agendas. Importantly, there are signs that the
politics of conflicting values will continue with or without Trump.[3]

The effects of the Trump era and the urban-rural divide are two important factors in explaining the successes and failures of women running state legislative campaigns. Contemporary research that focuses on
the political environment in which women run should be viewed as just
as consequential as research that focuses on gender explanations for the
lagging representation of women in US politics. The two worlds go hand
in hand in the current political climate and will probably shape future
elections cycles, especially for women. Any barriers that women still face
in politics do not exist in isolation from the political landscape in which
they are running. Our research affirms that when women run, they are

effective campaigners and are adept at understanding the political climate yet continue to be challenged by gender stereotypes.

By studying how women candidates have responded to the Trump effect and the urban-rural divide, we gain a better understanding of the institutional and societal barriers that may hinder rapid gains in the percentage of women serving in state legislatures. So long as hyperpartisanship and negative partisanship dominate US politics, successful female candidates will need to be a good fit for the districts they desire to represent.

Unlike previous former presidents, Trump did not go quietly into the night. His ongoing insistence that the election was rigged continues to fuel the fire among his most avid supporters. Recall that even in victory, Trump claimed that the 2016 election was rigged. Even then, Trump was tapping into an "us versus them" mentality among voters, reinforcing the tribal nature of US politics.[4] Embedded in the message was an emphasis on perceived real and imagined threats to the United States.[5] Trump's defeat in 2020 was not due to a rejection of his domestic policy agenda but rather to different personal attributes, as Biden "had a 22.5 point favorability rating over Trump and was safely in positive territory, that is nearly three times the favorability advantage held by Hillary Clinton in 2016."[6] Trump-era politics continues to affect state and local issues across the country. Republican-controlled state legislatures have prioritized changing election laws to reflect a belief that the system was corrupt. Conversely, Democrats argue that such laws are intended to prevent minorities and low-income citizens from voting. Division also arose over COVID-related policies that Republicans viewed as government overreach. In Democrat-controlled states, restrictions remained strong throughout. In Republican-controlled states, the preferred course of action, as stated by Governor Kim Reynolds of Iowa, was "to trust Iowans to do the right thing."[7] A third area of division centers around "culture wars" within the institution of US education.[8] A rising anger over what schools teach has fueled state legislatures to ban teaching of critical race theory and consider banning books on

LGBTQ-related topics.[9] Most notable is the Supreme Court decision to overturn *Roe v. Wade* in the *Dobbs v. Jackson Women's Health Organization* decision on June 24, 2022. Decisions related to reproductive rights now rest with the states and, in particular, with state legislatures. The results of the 2022 midterm election only serve to reinforce these divisions.[10] This presents unique challenges to state legislators that they may never have considered a reality and may further kindle the motive for women to run for state legislative office regardless of their position on the issue. The pink wave of women running for office may continue well into the future.

So long as hyperpartisanship and negative partisanship dominate US politics, successful female candidates will need to be a good fit for the districts they desire to represent. When we consider the urban-rural divide, it is clear that more conservative women will need to step forward and be supported by the Republican Party in rural areas. In urban areas, progressive women have a strong advantage. The most competitive seats for both parties will continue to be in suburban areas. Female candidates need to be found and groomed early and supported to enter the primaries in urban areas by Democrats and rural areas by Republicans. Party support, perhaps through subsidizing campaign staffers or start-up funding, could tip the scales toward more women running.[11] In the reddest of red and bluest of blue areas, the primaries become particularly important for candidates to compete in the current urban-rural political landscape. Strong party support of female candidates will need to occur early in the process, including a commitment to providing the resources needed to win the primary, with the realization that the primary winner will probably win the general election.

When we looked closer at the outcomes of state legislative races, we found a few situations in which election laws seemed to assist female candidates. We noted three instances in which women were elected from multirepresentative districts. Several respondents noted that term limits provided an opportunity to run in open seats rather than against an incumbent. Pettey has found that women are more likely to run for office in open seats created by term limits, a pattern that held true for both Republican and Democrat female candidates.[12] One concern regarding term-limited states is that the lack of experience works against becoming an effective legislator and could be a deterrent to running. Many states with term limits have beefed up their training and mentoring programs.[13] Female candidates concerned about being a successful legislator might find the professional development opportunities in term-limited states reassuring. The Nevada experience suggests that term limits contributed to the state becoming the first state legislative body that is more than 50 percent female.[14] One factor that needs further investigation is what constitutes term limits. There are fifteen states where legislators are term limited.[15] In ten of those states, a state legislator who has served the maximum-allowed consecutive terms in one legislative chamber may run for the other chamber.[16] Thus, term limits can be disguised to protect the staying power of the career politician. Without "real" term limits, those entrenched officeholders are more likely to be men. The impact of term limits on women running should be investigated further. Respondents in our survey who were first-time candidates, more often than not, were running in open seats. This is not to say that a person should not run in a district where one party or ideological slant is dominant. Research generally has not supported the notion that alternative election processes improve the odds of women winning elections. Is it possible that more women will run for office if they perceive that the system promotes a more level playing field?

There is plenty of evidence suggesting that women who consider running for office feel as though they need a certain level of self-confidence, rooted in a positive evaluation of their background and skill set, a healthy dose of political ambition, supportive encouragement from family and friends, and solid support from their political party. The current political climate, shaped by Trump-era politics, and the political geographic landscape, also impact the decision to run. A theme among respondents was a desire to create a collaborative legislative environment. Is a cooperative strategy possible in a culture-war environment? Candidates seeking to soften the tone may need additional encouragement and support to consider running for office in future election cycles. Obviously, prospective female candidates who fit comfortably in one of the cultural-war lanes might be less deterred by hostile politics.

As part of our research, we asked respondents what they considered most important when deciding to run for the state legislature as well as what they thought most impacted the outcome of their race. Additionally, in-depth interview participants were asked what advice they would give women about running for the state legislature. The responses to these questions yielded some fruitful advice to women candidates that we believe is important to share with those who may need some inspiration to encourage their candidacy.

Upon review of the responses provided by participants across two election cycles, we found that many still confronted stereotypes associated with women who run for office. Familial obligations often had to be weighed against the commitment to run and then serve, if elected. Several respondents reported confronting voters who wondered whether they had children and how they could manage both worlds. Teele et al. argue that women face a double standard when it comes to politics and family.[17] On the one hand, voters see family as a preferred quality in candidates. On the other hand, social expectations regarding caregiving responsibilities work against women who desire a career in politics. Teele et al. argue that successful female candidates must prove to voters that they can do both jobs well. Among our survey respondents were women who were empty-nesters or who reported having supportive partners willing and able to take on more caregiving responsibilities. While they could not prove a double standard, respondents questioned whether their male opponents would have to address as many family-oriented questions as they had to as female candidates. For instance, respondents wondered how many male candidates confront voters who ask, "Do you have children?"

Another finding from our research that remains consistent with the literature is the important role that the party plays in recruitment and in supporting the campaigns of female candidates. Unsurprisingly, respondents who reported winning their elections had fewer complaints about the adequacy of party support. One interesting piece of the connection between the party and the candidate was in the advice respondents had for women considering running for the state legislature. Many noted that women should first get involved in local and community-level politics. This advice may, unintentionally, reinforce the notion that women have to prepare more for political engagement than men do. Breaking the political glass ceiling remains problematic so long as local party organizations are dominated by male leadership. Further, many local parties rely on candidates emerging from more male-dominated professional backgrounds, such as law, business, or mayoral or city council experience.[18] The career patterns of respondents varied but trended more toward education and health-related fields. We found that, regardless of background, respondents possessed adequate skills to run and govern if elected. Nevertheless, as noted earlier, one respondent lamented the reality that the only thing a man needs to do to demonstrate his qualifications is to pick up a flag pen and sign the appropriate filing papers.

We found that, once on the campaign trail, women diverged on how they campaigned and the role of the party in their efforts. Respondents running in the suburbs tried to present themselves as moderates, while their opponents tried to paint them as extremists. In the most urban and rural areas, respondents who ran under the dominant party label were winning by large margins. For these women, the true test of their candidacy was in the primaries. In areas dominated by one party, the role of party elites becomes even more important to the recruitment of female candidates. Increasing the numbers of female state legislators may hinge on party efforts to find and support women candidates prior to and during the primary season.[19] This factor was reinforced by our examination of the urban-rural divide. In hindsight, we should have asked specific questions relating to the primary experience of respondents, although a few respondents did note the importance of the primaries to their overall campaign experience.

Respondents did not report feeling that gender stereotypes significantly impacted their ability to campaign. This finding is consistent with literature that shows that gender stereotypes have little impact on the win-loss rate of female candidates.[20] Ditonto and Anderson, however, are not willing to rule it out.[21] They contend that when multiple women are running for office, up and down the ballot, gender stereotypes seem to work against female candidates. As several respondents in our survey noted, it was quite typical for opposition candidates to link higher-level female politicians such as Nancy Pelosi to a female state legislative candidate, even though the two candidates had very little in common other than their party affiliation and their gender. Ads were slanted to paint the state legislative candidate as angry and unattractive, juxtaposing their image with that of former Speaker of the House Nancy Pelosi. Respondents reported difficulty getting their message across amid all of the fog created by the national political climate.

We know that the more time voters take to get to know a candidate, the more ordinary the candidate appears to be.[22] Candidates strive to be recognized for who they are as individuals and not stereotyped. Our research affirms that it would be unwise to rule out gender bias as an important variable in understanding the low representation of women in elected office. At the same time, respondents proved to be resilient and enthusiastic about campaigning for the state legislative seats they were seeking. They did not spend every moment on the campaign trail thinking about how gender would play into the outcome of their race. First and foremost, they campaigned as candidates and conducted themselves as professionals with a job to do, and they did it well, win or lose.

A common thread among respondents, whether they won or lost, was their desire to find ways to get more women involved in electoral politics. This perspective was built on the personal growth that many respondents reported because of having run for the state legislature. Often, respondents were clear about their disdain for the negative politics of the day. Nevertheless, for most of the respondents, the experience was of great personal value with regard to enhancing their professional and personal qualities. Thus, they began to see themselves as role models, hoping to inspire other women to get involved in politics. Interestingly, research suggests that the role-model effect on younger women is more powerful in areas where there have been fewer women running for office.[23] We find it encouraging that, despite the hostile political climate of current US politics, a majority of respondents reported that the positives of running far outweighed the negatives, and they wanted to pass along to potential candidates the enthusiasm generated by their experience. Hopefully, this book will assist in achieving that goal.

The recommendations suggested throughout this book emerged in the context of the hotly contested political climate of the times. What we have documented is the relationship between female candidates and the political landscape in which they had to operate during two chaotic election cycles. The political climate is just as real for women as it is for men, and it is often overlooked. We have written this book to share the experiences of women who ran for the state legislature during a turbulent political climate. It illustrates the intersectionality of political and social factors that will probably remain important in forthcoming election cycles. While women have a long road ahead of them to expand their numbers in state legislatures, we found that they were resilient and dedicated to closing the gap during and beyond the era of Trump.

Advice from Respondents to Women Considering Running for the State Legislature

Value of Involvement and Saying "Yes"

"Get involved in a local campaign so you understand how organizing works. Say yes to things. Take experiences as they come because you'll miss out if you don't."

"I would encourage all women to be involved as much as they can, in whatever manner you want to do it. Whether it's going to your city council meetings or PTA meetings. Because I was prepared, I was ready to serve. Build a network. That network will help you."

"If you are given an opportunity, you should accept it, even if you don't feel like you are in any way prepared to lead."

"I want to help educate [teens] and get them involved because statistically the younger you get a person involved in politics, the more likely they are going to stay engaged throughout their life."

"Although I lost, I am going all in with supporting other women who might run next time."

Know Yourself, Expectations, and When to Reach Out to Others

"You've got to be willing to be uncomfortable. You have to knock on doors and talk to total strangers. If you're not willing to do that, then you are not ready to run yet."

"You have to be willing to ask for help. You can't do it by yourself. Find people who are more experienced and get their help. You may have to pay for it. Don't begrudge paying someone for their expertise."

"Realize the importance of the different life experiences that women bring and the different leadership styles that women bring. We need more women of color and their life experiences."

Rewarding Experiences: Service Beyond Self

"I think there is value for people to step up and run even if they don't have a realistic chance of winning. The reason is to move the needle on dialog of what good government means and what our elected leaders should be doing. Also, if you don't run, you don't learn. I now know how much is involved in campaigning. With that knowledge, if I were to run again for something, I would know what I don't know. I would know how to recruit a team of people committed to helping with the campaign."

"This was an opportunity to grow myself outside of my career and a way to meet new people in my community that I probably wouldn't have otherwise."

"I needed to feel the work was purposeful and deep within my core. I had to feel connected to the work, the people, the reason, the outcome, and the larger picture."

"My participation in the process has been a remarkable experience. You will meet amazing people, constituents, who are amazing, and you hear amazing stories. That part of it is beyond rewarding. You learn not only about issues but how to work with people and how to bring people together."

"If you follow politics or an issue and you keep saying someone should do something, you are that someone. Don't wait for someone else to step up and do it. If you realistically cannot, for whatever reason—it's just not possible for you—find someone who can do it and just throw yourself into getting that person elected. If you want to see more women in government, then be that woman."

Realities of Work-Life Balance for Women

"We have to make it easier for anyone to run for office. Women are still expected to take care of the cooking, cleaning, and the child-care responsibilities. We need to get men to change so they are pulling their weight at home. A supportive partner is essential. If women had a good partner from day one, we would have more Ruth Bader Ginsburgs in the world."

"We were taught we can do it all. We can have a career and have someone else do the rest. We women are conditioned if we're not folding clothes, if we're not getting the kids the meals, or if we're not driving the carpool, it's on us. Women need to find a balance."

Next Steps: After the Election, What Does the Future Hold?
Among Those Who Lost

INVOLVEMENT

"I still want to be involved in some way. I want to do my best for the community. I have been appointed to two town committees. Also, there are a lot of young people, like me, who look at our representation and say, 'No

one cares what I have to say.' So I feel it's important for me to be there to
provide that different opinion that otherwise may not be heard."

"I am still on boards and committees and stay active in a nonprofit. If I don't
run again, I will actively recruit another woman to run."

"Honestly it was an impulsive move in 2018 in reaction to the worst president
and my own representative. Not a lot of consideration was had, but now
that I have built something, I am not sure where to go next, as I also lost in
2020. Ultimately my goal was to try and educate my community. So that
did happen. So more of that will hopefully be possible through the various
boards on which I currently sit."

POLITICAL GEOGRAPHY

"We are horribly gerrymandered. I anticipate they will try and further carve
out Democrats and make it a super-red stronghold. But you go into this
knowing you might lose. It's very rare to win all the elections you run in,
so you can't let that first loss keep you from running again. You do learn a
lot from your first race. I didn't win this one, but I will run again (maybe
a different district)."

"Right now I'm burnt out. I'm mad that my district and the entire state decided to go the other way."

From Those Who Won

UNITY

"I have three categories I want to pursue in my first term. The first is to work
on things that do not rely on Republican votes. Second, I want to be a
leader in my community and express values that we're all one community
together and should support one another. The last bucket are things I want
to advance even though we know they won't pass. Redistricting happens
in two years, so I have no idea what the future holds after that happens."

"I don't see doing this long term, maybe a couple of terms. I do want to retire
at some point. But for me, the mark of success will be the inclusiveness of
my district in terms of building a wholehearted community feel, like they

want to talk more and be involved more. I want to know how citizens really feel, and we need more people of color involved. I would like to foster that so we can look for a transition to more inclusiveness."

LOOKING FORWARD

"I will probably run again. How long does it take to be an effective legislator? It doesn't happen in the first two years. You spend your time learning and figuring things out. It is an ongoing process. We are going to be redistricted, so that factors into it also."

"Hopefully I will run again. I am looking to start a family this year. If that works out, I can still be ready for 2022. That's the plan today. Down the road, I would possibly run for state senate. I was actually tapped by the incumbent senator. He looked at the incoming freshman class of reps and asked, 'Who's going to replace me?' He said, 'It's going to have to be you,' and I haven't even started yet. But, yes, that is something I'm looking at."

"I got into politics because of how frustrated I was with the state of things. I don't actually know yet if doing this will make me more or less frustrated. Maybe I will be focused on simply doing the work, and I won't feel the aggravation. I don't want to make myself crazy by doing something like this."

ACKNOWLEDGMENTS

When we set out to explore why there was an increase in the number of women interested in running for state legislative office after the election of Donald J. Trump in 2016, we had no idea that the culmination of our research and writing would be centered around the phenomenon of what would eventually be referred to as the "Trump effect." As we gathered data in 2018, our sole focus was on the motivation of women running. As we prepared to send out the 2020 survey, the politically volatile environment was heating up and causing much havoc for candidates across the nation. Particularly for state legislative candidates in 2020, their campaigns were shaped by the national political climate. By the time of this publication, voters and candidates were finding national politics indistinguishable from local politics, and there is no sign that it will let up anytime soon. We wrote this book to appeal to an academic audience as well as a lay audience, including those running for office. Our hope is that you will enjoy reading it as much as we enjoyed writing it and that candidates, in particular, will be inspired by what these women experienced.

This book would not have been possible without significant assistance and support from several St. Ambrose University staff members and students. We would also like to extend our appreciation to researchers publishing in this area of women and politics, the CAWP, and the NCSL for answering our questions about their research and the data we were seeking. We would also like to thank St. Ambrose University for granting us a sabbatical to support our research and the time to work on this book.

We would be remiss if we did not thank our families for their support throughout this process. To our spouses, our children and their families, and our many other family, friends, and colleagues who have listened to us talk about this research since 2018, we thank you for listening and asking questions. We appreciate your patience, understanding, and encouragement throughout the writing of this book.

METHODOLOGICAL APPENDIX

In 2018, we sent two surveys to all women running for the state legislature during the midterm election. One survey was sent prior to the election, and the other survey was sent after the election. In 2020, we decided to combine the essence of the two surveys we sent in 2018 into one. We sent out the email with the survey link on the Saturday following the general election in 2020. We contemplated the benefits and costs of combining two surveys into one. Feedback from 2018 survey respondents suggested that being asked to complete two surveys was too time-consuming, and we observed a significant drop in participation in the 2018 postelection survey. The survey we sent in 2020 was initially sent within days of the general election. The response rate was lower than we expected, and after some reflection, we believe we should have sent emails with the 2020 survey link the weekend prior to the election. We suspect that many candidates, especially those who lost their races, may not have continued to consistently check the email associated with their candidacy over the days following their race. Additionally, we were informed from many of our respondents that they received multiple surveys from researchers during the 2020 election cycle.

Prior to sending any emails with survey links in 2018, we secured an email address from the university solely for this research project. This helped us to filter messages and easily eliminate auto-reply messages from candidates without flooding our personal university email inboxes. We worked with the university communications and marketing office to send a bulk email using campaign manager software. This allowed us to send the survey link to a large number of email addresses and to readily access data analytics typically reported when using such software.

An analysis follows that summarizes the number of emails sent in 2018 and 2020 as well as the survey clicks associated with the emails opened. The high number of emails opened and links clicked in 2018 and in 2020, when compared to the number of surveys we received, may suggest that candidates had campaign fatigue or were overwhelmed with the number of surveys received. As well, for the 2020 survey, not capturing the attention of candidates in the days prior to the 2020 election may have negatively influenced whether candidates opened the email and clicked on the survey link.

In 2018, we had a team of students and staff at St. Ambrose who worked with us to identify women running for state legislative seats in the forty-six states holding a midterm election. We started identifying candidates and their email addresses a little later than we should have and worked from early September 2018 until we sent the email and survey link on October 16, 2018. For the email and survey link sent in 2020, we began gathering names of candidates as soon as the secretary of state office in the forty-four states holding state legislative races posted their district candidates following state primary results for the general election. We began this process in the spring of 2020. It is worth noting the inconsistencies among the states in the information they publish regarding state legislative candidates and their contact information. Most states do not provide contact information for the candidates running, so that information was sought through multiple resources including candidates' campaign webpages, Facebook pages, state government webpages (for those who were incumbents), ballotpedia.org, and justfacts .votesmart.org. We exhausted all resources to put together a comprehensive list of state legislative candidates and their contact information for both 2018 and 2020. Therefore, the number of emails we sent differs from the number of women running, due to the inability to find email contact information as well as the duplication of email addresses associated with a candidate.

We acquired a significant amount of data from open-ended questions for the 2018 and 2020 surveys. As a result, we decided to conduct virtual in-depth interviews following the 2020 survey with select interested candidates. From the 2020 survey, there were 208 survey participants (out of 221 total) who indicated their willingness to participate in an in-depth interview. Because it would be an unnecessary and monumental task to engage in an in-depth interview with all of the willing participants, we decided to begin first with those who were rebound candidates (ran in 2018, lost, and then ran again in 2020). Reaching out to rebound candidates provided an opportunity to explore, in-depth, factors motivating them to run, including the influence of the national political climate on their decision to run a second time. There were thirty-seven candidates who completed the survey who identified as a rebound candidate. We reached out to them, and fourteen agreed to be interviewed. Because the most competitive seats are found in suburban districts, the next round of survey participants we wanted to interview were those who ran and won in the suburbs.[1] We reached out to twenty-six survey participants who ran and won in the suburbs, and eight agreed to be interviewed. We stayed away from interviewing candidates from safe districts (often urban or rural), opting instead to focus on candidates in competitive races, as we sought a fuller picture of the campaign landscape. The remaining interviews were conducted with women who ran for the first time and won in their district. We conducted a total of twenty-three virtual in-depth interviews between December 1, 2020, and January 18, 2021.

Readers may notice discrepancies in how we reported demographics for participants who have been quoted throughout the book. In order to protect the identity of certain participants who may easily be identified, it did not seem prudent to identify the state, party affiliation, date, or election outcome when reporting their experiences. We were concerned that, given the political geography of where some of the candidates campaigned, these demographic identifiers could be used to trace some respondents. For example, a few respondents ran in states that were dominated by one political party, and we determined that identifying the state could easily reveal these respondents' identity if someone were inclined to investigate. In these instances, we decided to refer to the region where the candidate/respondent resided, such as Great Plains, Mountain West, or Northeast. Additionally, several questions were designed to explore the respondents' general campaign experience, and when we reported their experiences in relation to those questions, it seemed that reporting the state, political party affiliation, year, or outcome of the race was not central to the point we were trying to convey when documenting the account of their experience. Great care was taken to ensure that we were reporting only what was necessary and what we had specified in our informed consent statement to protect the identity of participants.

TABLE A.1. Campaign Monitor Summary of Emails Sent, with Survey Link, Emails Opened, and the Number of Associated Clicks in 2018 and 2020

Campaign Monitor emails sent in 2018	Date sent	Number of emails sent*	Opens** (percentage reflects those opened minus bounce-backs)	Clicks (total response rate)
Survey 1, 2018, initial send	Tuesday, Oct. 16, 2018 3:30 p.m.	3,952	1,675 (45.69%)	354 (21.13%)
Follow-up email for survey 1	Tuesday, Oct. 23, 2018 9:00 a.m.	3,411	1,120 (33.8%)	146 (13.04%)
Survey 2, 2018 (postelection survey), initial send	Friday, Nov. 9, 2018 6:30 p.m.	3,745	1,438 (39.58%)	276 (19.19%)
Follow-up email for survey 2	Wednesday, Nov. 14, 2018 6:15 p.m.	3,477	890 (26.44%)	86 (9.66%)
Campaign Monitor emails sent in 2020				
Initial email	Saturday Nov. 7, 2020 9:00 a.m.	3,148	1,001 (33.9%)	204 (20.3%)
Follow-up email	Wednesday Nov. 11, 2020 12:10 p.m.	3,096	978 (32.8%)	167 (17.07%)
Third follow-up email	Wednesday Nov. 18, 2020 7:00 p.m.	2,947	834 (29.5%)	127 (15.22%)

* For candidates who had multiple emails available, duplicate emails were sent.
** The industry-standard click rate for nonprofit organizations is 28 percent (Cahoon, 2021).

Women Running for State Legislature	

Initial Survey
Women Running for State Legislature

You have been sent this survey to consider completing because you are a female who is either currently serving in a state legislative seat or are on the 2018 ballot for a state legislative seat. We are faculty from St. Ambrose University in Davenport, Iowa and have a strong interest in understanding what influenced or is impacting you to consider a run for the state legislature. If you would take a few minutes to respond to the following questions we would greatly appreciate your input. Your responses will remain confidential. By completing the survey you are consenting to participate in the research. Thank you in advance for your time.
Regina Matheson, PhD. and William Parsons, PhD.

1. What is your political party affiliation?

◯ Democrat   ◯ Independent

◯ Republican

◯ Other (please specify)

[   ]

2. Which of the following best describes your political ideology?

Liberal   Moderate   Conservative

3. What is your age?

[   ]

4. What is your race/ethnicity?

◯ American Indian or Alaskan Native   ◯ Hispanic or Latino

◯ Asian   ◯ Native Hawaiian or Pacific Islander

◯ Black/African American   ◯ White/Caucasian

◯ Other (please specify)

[   ]

FIGURE A.1. Initial survey, 2018

5. Are you currently

◯ Married

◯ Single

◯ Divorced/seperated

◯ Widowed

Other (please specify)

[   ]

6. Do you have (check all that apply)

◯ children 10 and younger   ◯ children older than 18 not in the home

◯ children ages 11-18   ◯ I have no children

◯ children older than 18 and still at home

◯ Other (please specify)

[   ]

7. Have you ever served in an elected office?

◯ Yes   ◯ No

If you are currently serving or have served in an elected office, what is/was your position?

[   ]

8. Are you running for a state legislative seat for the first time?

◯ Yes

◯ No

9. Are you an incumbent running again for a state legislative seat?

◯ Yes

◯ No

10. If you are currently serving in a state legislative seat and have decided to NOT run for re-election, why?

[   ]

11. In which state are you running for state legislature?

[   ]

12. What is the number associated with your district?

[   ]

13. Would you categorize the district in which you are running as mostly?

Urban   Suburban   Rural

14 How far in miles is your home from your state capitol?

15. Do you consider the district/seat you are running for as?

○ Competitive

○ Non Competitive

○ I am running unopposed

16. How did you consider the following factors in your decision to run for State Legislature?

	Not at all important	Low importance	Neutral	Moderately important	Extremely important
The outcome of the 2016 Presidential election	○	○	○	○	○
Your proximity to your state capitol	○	○	○	○	○
The number of women currently in state and federal offices	○	○	○	○	○
The percentage of your preferred political party represented in state and federal elected seats	○	○	○	○	○
The percentage of OTHER political parties represented in state and federal elected seats	○	○	○	○	○
The current political climate in the country	○	○	○	○	○
Possessing a suitable skill set for an elected office	○	○	○	○	○
Desire to learn about the issues you would face in the state legislature	○	○	○	○	○
The desire to become more civically engaged	○	○	○	○	○
The "Me Too" Movement	○	○	○	○	○
The Women's Marches across the country	○	○	○	○	○
The competitiveness of your district seat	○	○	○	○	○
Campaign financing support	○	○	○	○	○
You have a male opponent	○	○	○	○	○
You have a female opponent	○	○	○	○	○

17. What other factors did you consider when running for the state legislature?

18. From your perspective, what are the most important factors for women to consider as they prepare to run for office?

19. Did you initiate the process of running for state legislative office or were you recruited? Please elaborate.

20. Do you feel as though you got satisfactory support from your political party? Please elaborate.

○ Yes   ○ Not sure

○ No

Please elaborate

21. Is there anything you would like to add that we didn't ask?

Post Election Survey
Women running for State Legislature

Post Election Survey
Women running for State Legislature

You have been sent this post mid-term election survey as a follow-up to the survey you were sent in October regarding women running for state legislature. We are interested in understanding your experience as you ran for a state legislative seat. We again appreciate your willingness to complete this post election survey. If you would take a few minutes to respond to the following questions we would greatly appreciate your input. Your responses will remain confidential. By completing the survey you are consenting to participate in the research. Thank you in advance for your time.
Regina Matheson, PhD. and William Parsons, PhD.

1. What is your political party affiliation?

- ◯ Democrat
- ◯ Republican
- ◯ Independent
- ◯ Other (please specify) [ ]
- ◯ Libertarian
- ◯ Green Party

2. Which of the following best describes your political ideology?

Liberal — Moderate — Conservative [ ]

3. What is your age?

[ ]

4. What is your race/ethnicity?

- ◯ American Indian or Alaskan Native
- ◯ Asian
- ◯ Black/African American
- ◯ Other (please specify) [ ]
- ◯ Hispanic or Latino
- ◯ Native Hawaiian or Pacific Islander
- ◯ White/Caucasian

FIGURE A.2. Postelection survey, 2018

5. Are you currently

○ Married   ○ Widowed

○ Single   ○ Cohabitating

○ Divorced/seperated

Other (please specify)

[   ]

6. Are you caring for (check all that apply)

○ children 10 and younger   ○ relatives not living in your home

○ children ages 11-18   ○ relatives living in your home

○ children older than 18 and still at home   ○ I am not caring for children or other relatives

○ children older than 18 not in the home

Other (please specify)

[   ]

7. What is the highest level of education you have completed?

○ Less than a high school diploma   ○ Associates degree

○ High school graduate/GED   ○ Bachelors degree

○ Some college   ○ Graduate degree

8. Were you an incumbent running again for a state legislative seat?

○ Yes

○ No

9. Was this election the first time you ran for elected office?

○ Yes

○ No

10. In which state did you run for state legislature?

[   ]

11. What is the number associated with your district?

[   ]

12. Would you categorize the district in which you ran as mostly?

Urban   Suburban   Rural

○─── [   ]

13. Was your seat a competitive seat (won or lost by 3% or less)?

◯ Yes

◯ No

◯ I ran unopposed

14. Did you win the election?

◯ Yes   ◯ No

15. How do you consider the following factors in the outcome of your state legislative race?

	Not at all important	Low importance	Neutral	Moderately important	Extremely important
What is happening in the national political scene	○	○	○	○	○
What is happening in your statewide political arena	○	○	○	○	○
What is happening within your political district	○	○	○	○	○
The quality of your opponent in the election	○	○	○	○	○
Your prior elected office experience	○	○	○	○	○
Your professional experience	○	○	○	○	○
Your prior campaign experience	○	○	○	○	○
Adequate financing to support your campaign	○	○	○	○	○
Adequate support from your political party to support your campaign	○	○	○	○	○
You had a female opponent	○	○	○	○	○
You had a male opponent	○	○	○	○	○
Your sex/gender	○	○	○	○	○
Voter turnout in your district	○	○	○	○	○
Your opportunities to connect with voters	○	○	○	○	○

Other (please specify)

16. What factors do you think MOST impacted your state legislative race? Please elaborate

17. What, if anything, would you have done differently regarding your race for a state legislative seat?

18. If you won your election how do you plan to negotiate work/life balance now that you will be serving in the state legislature?

19. Is there anything you would like to add that we didn't ask?

2020 Women running for State Legislature

Women running for the State Legislature in 2020

You have been sent this survey to consider completing because you are a woman running for a state legislative seat in the 2020 general election for your state. We are faculty from St. Ambrose University in Davenport, Iowa conducting research on women running for state legislative seats in their respective state. Our goal is to publish a book that focuses on women who ran for state legislative seats in the 2018 mid-term election and the 2020 general election. There is a lack of literature on the motivation of women to run for state legislative office, and these two elections have much history to contribute in this area. The questions that follow relate to your decision to run for office as well as the outcome of your race. The survey will take about 25 minutes to complete. We understand that this is a VERY busy time for you as you have been campaigning and wrapping up your election, but if you would take a few minutes to respond to this survey, we would greatly appreciate your input. Your responses will remain confidential. By completing this survey, you are consenting to participate in this research. Thank you in advance for your time. Regina Matheson, PhD. and William Parsons, PhD.

1. What is your political party affiliation?

- ◯ Republican
- ◯ Democrat
- ◯ Independent
- ◯ Libertarian
- ◯ Green Party

Other (please specify)

[   ]

2. Which of the following best describes your political ideology?

Liberal　　　　　　　　　　　　Moderate　　　　　　　　　　　　Conservative

3. What is your age?

[   ]

4. What is your race/ethnicity (check all that apply)?

- ☐ White or Caucasian
- ☐ Black or African American
- ☐ Hispanic or Latino
- ☐ Asian or Asian American
- ☐ American Indian or Alaska Native
- ☐ Native Hawaiian or other Pacific Islander
- ☐ Another race

Other (please specify)

[   ]

FIGURE A.3. Survey, 2020

5. What is your relationship status (check all that apply)?

☐ Married

☐ Single

☐ Divorced/separated

☐ Widowed

☐ Cohabitating

☐ Engaged

Other (please specify)

[   ]

6. What is the highest level of school you have completed or the highest degree you have received?

○ Less than high school diploma

○ High school degree or equivalent (e.g., GED)

○ Some college but no degree

○ Associate degree

○ Bachelor degree

○ Graduate degree

7. Are you caring for (check all that apply)?

☐ children younger than 18   ☐ aging or other relatives not living in your home

☐ children 18 or older still living at home ☐ aging or other relatives living in your home

☐ children older than 18 not in the home   ☐ I am not caring for children or other relatives

8. If you are elected to serve will you?

○ Make this role your primary work responsibility

○ Balance a job or other professional role while serving

9. Which of the following best describes your current occupation?

- ◯ Management Occupations
- ◯ Business and Financial Operations Occupations
- ◯ Computer and Mathematical Occupations
- ◯ Architecture and Engineering Occupations
- ◯ Life, Physical, and Social Science Occupations
- ◯ Community and Social Service Occupations
- ◯ Legal Occupations
- ◯ Education, Training, and Library Occupations
- ◯ Arts, Design, Entertainment, Sports, and Media Occupations
- ◯ Healthcare Practitioners and Technical Occupations
- ◯ Healthcare Support Occupations
- ◯ Protective Service Occupations
- ◯ Food Preparation and Serving Related Occupations
- ◯ Building and Grounds Cleaning and Maintenance Occupations
- ◯ Personal Care and Service Occupations
- ◯ Sales and Related Occupations
- ◯ Office and Administrative Support Occupations
- ◯ Farming, Fishing, and Forestry Occupations
- ◯ Construction and Extraction Occupations
- ◯ Installation, Maintenance, and Repair Occupations
- ◯ Production Occupations
- ◯ Transportation and Materials Moving Occupations
- ◯ Other (please specify)

```

```

10. In 2020, are you running for a state legislative seat for the first time?

- ◯ Yes
- ◯ No

11. Did you run for a state legislative seat in 2018?

- ◯ Yes
- ◯ No

12. If you answered yes to the previous question, did you win or lose the race in 2018?

○ Won

○ Lost

○ I didn't run in 2018

13. Are you an Incumbent running again in 2020 for a state legislative seat?

○ Yes

○ No

14. In which state are you running for the state legislature?

[   ]

15. What is the number associated with the state district in which you are running?

[   ]

16. What is the state and number of the congressional district in which you are running? (for example IA-02)

[   ]

17. How far in miles is your home from the state capitol?

[   ]

18. How do you consider the district/seat for which you are running?

○ Competitive

○ Non Competitive

○ I am running unopposed

19. How would you categorize the district in which you are running?

Urban   Suburban   Rural

○━━━━━━━━━━━━━━━━━━━━━━━━━━━━━━━━━━━━━━━   [   ]

20. How did you consider the following factors in your decision to run for the State Legislature?

	Extremely Important	Moderately Important	Neutral	Low Importance	Not at all Important	Not Applicable
Being a primary caregiver to family members	○	○	○	○	○	○
Balancing the elected role with a professional occupation	○	○	○	○	○	○
How far you live from the state capitol	○	○	○	○	○	○
Ability to manage your household while serving in office	○	○	○	○	○	○
Running for a competitive seat	○	○	○	○	○	○
Running in an area that generally supports the opposing party	○	○	○	○	○	○
Having negative ads run about you	○	○	○	○	○	○
Your sex/gender as an asset to winning	○	○	○	○	○	○

21. From question 20 above, what are the top 3 factors you think MOST impacted your decision to run for the state legislature? Please elaborate.

22. How did you consider the following factors in your decision to run for the State Legislature?

	Extremely Important	Moderately Important	Neutral	Low Importance	Not at all Important	Not Applicable
Longstanding desire to be in politics	○	○	○	○	○	○
Recent desire to be in politics	○	○	○	○	○	○
The state legislative seat was an important stepping stone toward another higher office	○	○	○	○	○	○
Having a suitable skills set and qualifications for the position	○	○	○	○	○	○
Coming from an occupational background that has typically lead to a career in politics (i.e. business and law)	○	○	○	○	○	○
Coming from an occupational background that has NOT typically lead to a career in politics	○	○	○	○	○	○
Confidence in winning the seat	○	○	○	○	○	○
Encouragement from your political party to run	○	○	○	○	○	○
Encouragement from others outside your political party to run	○	○	○	○	○	○
The increase in the number of women running for and elected to office since 2016	○	○	○	○	○	○

23. All things considered, why did you decide to run for the state legislature in 2020?

24. How did you campaign for your election?

25. How was your decision to run and your campaign impacted by COVID 19?

26. What other factors did you consider when running for the State Legislature?

27. Did you initiate the process of running for state legislative office or were you recruited? Please elaborate.

28. Did you win the election?

○ Yes

○ No

29. Was your seat a competitive seat (won or lost by 3% or less)?

○ Yes

○ No

○ I ran unopposed

30. How do you consider the following factors in the outcome of your state legislative race?

	Extremely Important	Moderately Important	Neutral	Low Importance	Not at all Important	Not Applicable
What is happening in the national political scene	○	○	○	○	○	○
What is happening in your statewide political arena	○	○	○	○	○	○
What is happening within your local political district	○	○	○	○	○	○
Your prior elected office experience	○	○	○	○	○	○
Your professional experience	○	○	○	○	○	○
Your prior campaign experience	○	○	○	○	○	○
Adequate financing to support your campaign	○	○	○	○	○	○
How you had to campaign because of COVID-19	○	○	○	○	○	○
Adequate support from your political party to assist with your campaign	○	○	○	○	○	○
Your sex/gender	○	○	○	○	○	○
Voter turnout in your district	○	○	○	○	○	○
Inadequate opportunities to connect face to face with voters	○	○	○	○	○	○
The competitiveness of your district seat	○	○	○	○	○	○

31. From question 27 above, what are the top 3 factors you think MOST impacted the outcome of your state legislative race? Please elaborate.

32. What, if anything, would you have done differently regarding your race for a state legislative seat? Please elaborate.

33. From your perspective, what are the most important factors that women have to consider as they prepare to run for office? Please elaborate.

34. Is there anything you would like to add that we didn't ask?

35. We would be delighted to follow up with anyone willing to engage in an in-depth interview about your experience running for office. You can leave your name and contact information here or email us at statelegislatureresearch@sau.edu

Name

State/Province   -- select state --

Email Address

Phone Number

IN-DEPTH INTERVIEW QUESTIONS/GUIDE 2020

Date: _____ Time:_____ Political Party: _____

Person Interviewed:_____ Consent to be interviewed/re-corded: _____

From State: _____ Ran in 2018: YES   NO

In 2020: WON LOST

1. Why did you decide to run for the state legislature? Elaborate on your experience(s) you have had as you lead up to making this decision as well as the experiences you have had since making this decision. (If you also ran in 2018, how would you compare your experiences to 2020, why did you decide to run again)?

2. Describe your district (if haven't already).

3. Do you think the national political climate impacted your 2020 race? If you ran in 2018, how would you compare the two?

4. Describe how campaigning this year amidst COVID impacted your race.

5. Did you seek out and/or participate in any candidate professional development programs?

6. Did you have any experiences that you think may have been unique to you as a female candidate?

7. What advice would you give to other women as they run for office?

8. Where do you go from here?

NOTES

CHAPTER 1. SHE RUNS

1. CAWP, 2022a, 2022b, 2022c, 2023a, 2023b; Congressional Research Service, 2022; Blazina and Desilver, 2021.
2. CAWP, 2022b, 2022c; Hinchliffe, Bellstrom, and Zillman, 2018.
3. Zhou, 2018; Herrnson, Lay, and Stokes, 2003.
4. CAWP, 2019b; CAWP, 2020c.
5. Tumulty, 2018.
6. Carpini and Fuchs, 1993.
7. Dimock and Wike, 2020.
8. Dyck, Pearson-Merkowitz, and Coates, 2018.
9. Williams, 2015; Jacobson, 2016; La Raja and Rauch, 2020; Hopkins, 2022; Eberly, 2022; Tichenor and Fuerstman, 2008.
10. CAWP, 2019a.
11. CAWP, 2020b.
12. Stewart, 2019.
13. CAWP, 2019b.
14. CAWP, 2020c.
15. Dittmar, 2020b.
16. Sides et al., 2019.
17. Lawless and Fox, 2017.
18. Costello, 2016; Lawless and Fox, 2018.
19. Fiorina, 2017.
20. Frey, 2020; Gabriel, 2020; Skelley and Wiederkehr, 2021.
21. O'Neill, 1995.
22. Hopkins, 2018.
23. Dittmar, 2017; Bystrom, 2018.
24. Enli and Moe, 2017.
25. Snyder, 2020.

CHAPTER 2. DECIDING TO RUN

1. Costello, 2016.
2. Kivisto, 2017, p. 6.
3. Haberman, 2021; Jefferson, 2021.
4. Newman et al., 2020, p. 1156.

5. Lawless and Fox, 2018.

6. Sword and Zimbardo, 2018; Costello, 2016.

7. Kamarck, Podkul, and Zeppos, 2018.

8. Alter, 2018; Dittmar, 2019; Hayes, 2018; Lawless and Fox, 2018.

9. Tumulty, 2018.

10. Lawless and Fox, 2018.

11. Fox and Lawless, 2014a; Johnson and Stanwick, 1976; Stalsburg, 2012; Sanbonmatsu, Carroll, and Walsh, 2009.

12. Sanbonmatsu, 2018.

13. Schlesinger, 1966; Black, 1972; Levine and Hyde, 1977; Bledsoe and Herring, 1990; Fulton et al., 2006; Fox and Lawless, 2010.

14. Fulton et al., 2006; Clark, Hadley, and Darcy, 1989; Fox and Lawless, 2004; Sanbonmatsu, 2002.

15. Pearson and McGhee, 2013.

16. Carroll and Sanbonmatsu, 2013.

17. Holman and Schneider, 2018.

18. Carroll and Sanbonmatsu, 2013.

19. Sanbonmatsu, Carroll, and Walsh, 2009.

20. Holman and Schneider, 2018; Dolan and Hansen, 2018.

21. Fox and Lawless, 2010.

22. Clark, 1994; Fox and Lawless, 2004; Niven, 2006; Francis and Kenny, 2000.

23. Dolan and Ford, 1997.

24. Sanbonmatsu, 2002.

25. Fox and Lawless, 2010.

26. Sanbonmatsu, Carroll, and Walsh, 2009.

27. Fox and Lawless, 2011; Lawless and Fox, 2010; Wolak, 2020.

28. Sanbonmatsu, Carroll, and Walsh, 2009.

29. Elsesser, 2019.

30. Coury et al., 2020.

31. Eagly and Steffen, 1984; Storage et al., 2020.

32. Eder and Parker 1987; Eder, Evans, and Parker, 1995; Charles and Bradley, 2009; Mohr, 2014.

33. Fulton, 2012.

34. Branton et al., 2018; Carnevale, Smith, and Peltier-Campbell, 2019.

35. Lawless, 2015; Lorber, 2018.

36. Guillen, 2018; Fox and Lawless, 2014b; Kay and Shipman, 2014; Vajapey, Weber, and Samora, 2020.

37. Oliver and Conroy, 2020.

38. Pew Research Center, 2013.

39. Carroll and Sanbonmatsu, 2013; Stalsburg, 2010.

40. Sanbonmatsu, Carroll, and Walsh, 2009.

41. Johnson and Stanwick, 1976.
42. National Alliance for Caregiving, 2020.
43. Coury et al., 2020.
44. Hochschild and Machung, 2012; Elder, 2004; Silbermann, 2015a, 2015b.
45. Sayer, 2005; Sayer et al., 2009.
46. Fox and Lawless, 2014a.
47. Silbermann, 2015a.
48. Oliver and Conroy, 2020.
49. Dittmar, 2020b.

CHAPTER 3. MAKING HISTORY

1. Alter, 2018.
2. Lawless and Fox, 2018.
3. CAWP, 2021a.
4. Dolan and Shah, 2020.
5. Goodkind, 2018; Haslett, 2018.
6. Oliver and Conroy, 2020; Schnell, 2019; Ditonto and Anderson, 2018.
7. Dolan and Shah, 2020.
8. Vallejo, 2019.
9. CAWP, 2021c.
10. CAWP 2021d.
11. CAWP, 2020b.
12. Juenke et al., 2020.
13. Catalyst, 2021.
14. Juenke et al., 2020.
15. CAWP, 2021d.
16. Shah, 2014; Juenke and Shah, 2016; Juenke et al., 2020.
17. Thomsen-DeVeaux and Conroy, 2020.
18. Silva and Skulley, 2018; Frederick 2013.
19. Holman and Schneider, 2018.
20. Carroll and Sanbonmatsu, 2013.
21. Carroll and Sanbonmatsu, 2013.
22. Carroll and Sanbonmatsu, 2013.
23. Silva and Skulley, 2018.
24. Silva and Skulley, 2018.
25. Dungca et al., 2020.
26. Alter, 2020.
27. Kaplan, 2020.
28. Ramirez, 2020.
29. Morrison, 2020.
30. Perry 2018.

31. Shah, Scott, and Juenke, 2019.
32. Carroll and Sanbonmatsu, 2013; Perry, 2018.

CHAPTER 4. RUNNING FOR STATE LEGISLATURE

1. Desilver, 2013; Fiorina, 2017.
2. Galvin, Schlozman, and Rosenfeld, 2020.
3. Cook, 2020; Lach, 2020; Tavernise, 2020.
4. Stahl, 2021.
5. Pew Research Center, 2020.
6. Rakich, 2020a.
7. Miller, 2016; Steinhauer, 2019.
8. Bystrom, 2018.
9. Butler and Preece, 2016.
10. Erler, 2018.
11. Herrnson, 2009.
12. Sides et al., 2019.
13. Bacon, 2018; Shames, 2018.
14. Elder, 2018; Thomsen, 2018; Dittmar, 2018.
15. Wineinger, 2018.
16. Pierucci, 2020.
17. Shames, 2015.
18. Pierucci, 2020.
19. Bacon, 2018; Och, 2018.
20. Shames, 2015, p. 3.
21. Shames, 2015, p. 4.
22. Emily's List, 2021.
23. Shames, 2015.
24. Pierucci, 2020; Shames, 2015.
25. Hogan, 2007.
26. Montemayor and Quist, 2020; Evers-Hillstrom and Haley, 2020.
27. Sanbonmatsu, Carroll, and Walsh, 2009.
28. CAWP, 2020a.
29. Krupnikov and Bauer, 2013.
30. Kanthak and Woon, 2015.
31. Herrnson, Lay, and Stokes, 2003.
32. Schneider et al., 2016; Parker, Horowitz, and Igielnik, 2018.
33. Pusateri, 2020.
34. Manchester, 2020; Simon, 2020; Power, 2020.
35. Bystrom et al., 2004; Dolan, 2005; Herrnson, Lay, and Stokes, 2003.
36. Dittmar, 2015; Dolan and Lynch, 2017.

CHAPTER 5. THE URBAN-RURAL DIVIDE

1. Bacon, 2021.
2. Demore, Lan, and Danielson, 2018, 2021; Ajilore, 2020; Florida, 2020; Florida, Patino, and Dottle, 2020; Gimpel, Lovin, and Reeves, 2020; Kanik and Scott, 2020; Rakich, 2020b, Montgomery, 2018; Dottle and Druke, 2018.
3. Savat, 2020.
4. Hendrix, 2020.
5. Florida, 2020.
6. Gimpel, Lovin, and Reeves, 2020.
7. Leatherby, 2016.
8. Fiorina, 2017.
9. Fiorina, 2017, p. 74.
10. Hendrix, 2020.
11. Lu and Yourish, 2020.
12. Frey, 2020; Florida et al., 2020; Skelley et al., 2020.
13. Montgomery, 2020.
14. Florida and Montgomery, 2018; Montgomery, 2018.
15. Florida and Montgomery, 2018.
16. Florida and Montgomery, 2018.
17. Demographic Statistical Atlas of the United States, 2021.
18. Demographic Statistical Atlas of the United States, 2021.
19. Florida and Montgomery, 2018.
20. Ballotpedia, 2021.
21. Votesmart, 2021.
22. Ballotpedia, 2021.
23. Ballotpedia, 2021.
24. Ballotpedia, 2021.
25. Ballotpedia, 2021; Demographic Statistical Atlas of the United States, 2021.
26. Demographic Statistical Atlas of the United States, 2021.
27. Ballotpedia, 2021.
28. Ballotpedia, 2021.
29. Ballotpedia, 2021.
30. Ballotpedia, 2021.
31. Elder, 2018.
32. Elder, 2018.
33. Dittmar, 2020a.
34. Gimpel, Lovin, and Reeves, 2020.
35. Abramowitz and Webster, 2018.
36. Drutman, 2021.

CHAPTER 6. EXPANDING THE RANKS

1. Busch, 2022.
2. O'Neill, 1995.
3. Busch, 2022.
4. French, 2020.
5. MacWilliams, 2016.
6. Eberly, 2022, p. 14.
7. Office of the Governor of Iowa Kim Reynolds, 2021.
8. Smith, 2021; Zimmerman, 2021.
9. Ray and Gibbons, 2021; Clayworth, 2022.
10. Luthra, 2022; Yurcaba, 2023.
11. Krook and Norris, 2014.
12. Pettey, 2017.
13. Kurtz, 2021.
14. Snyder, 2020.
15. Kurtz, 2021.
16. Ballotpedia, 2021.
17. Teele, Kalla, and Rosenbluth, 2018.
18. Crowder-Meyer, 2013.
19. Niven, 2006; Conroy and Rakich, 2020.
20. Brooks, 2013; Dolan, 2014; Hayes, 2011.
21. Ditonto and Andersen, 2018.
22. Ditonto and Andersen, 2018.
23. Wolbrecht and Campbell, 2017.

METHODOLOGICAL APPENDIX

1. Frey, 2020; Gabriel, 2020; Skelley and Wiederkehr, 2021.

REFERENCES

Abramowitz, A., and Webster, S. (2018). Negative partisanship: Why Americans dislike parties but behave like rabid partisans. *Political Psychology*, 39(3), 119–135.

Ajilore, O. (2020, December 22). The role of rural communities of color in the 2020 election. Center for American Progress. www.americanprogress.org.

Alter, C. (2018, January 18). A year ago they marched. Now a record number of women are running for office. *Time*. https://time.com.

Alter, C. (2020, June 17). How Black Lives Matter could reshape the 2020 elections. *Time*. https://time.com.

Bacon, P. (2018, June 25). Why the Republican Party elects so few women. *FiveThirtyEight*. https://fivethirtyeight.com.

Bacon, P. (2021, February 16). The Trumpiest Republicans are at the state and local levels. *FiveThirtyEight*. https://fivethirtyeight.com.

Ballotpedia. (2021). Ballotpedia's candidate survey. https://ballotpedia.org.

Black, G. (1972). A theory of political ambition: Career choices and the role of structural incentives. *American Political Science Review*, 66(1), 144–159.

Blazina, C., and Desilver, D. (2021, January 15). A record number of women are serving in the 117th Congress. Pew Research Center. www.pewresearch.org.

Bledsoe, T., and Herring, M. (1990). Victims of circumstances: Women in pursuit of political office. *American Political Science Review*, 84(1), 213–223.

Branton, R., English, A., Pettey, S., and Barnes, T. (2018). The impact of gender and quality opposition on the relative assessment of candidate competency. *Electoral Studies*, 54, 35–43.

Brooks, D. (2013). *He runs, she runs: Why gender stereotypes do not harm women candidates*. Princeton, NJ: Princeton University Press.

Burrell, B. (2018). Political parties and women's organizations: Bringing women into the electoral process. In S. Carroll and R. Fox (Eds.), *Gender and elections: Shaping the future of American politics*, 4th ed. (pp. 220–249). New York: Cambridge University Press.

Busch, A. (2022). Domestic policy legacies of the Trump presidency. In S. Schier and T. Eberly (Eds.), *The Trump effect* (pp. 125–145). Lanham, MD: Rowman and Littlefield.

Butler, D., and Preece, J. (2016). Recruitment and gender bias in party leader support. *Political Research Quarterly*, 69(4), 842–851.

Bystrom, D. (2018). Gender and communication on the campaign trail: Media coverage, advertising, and online outreach. In S. Carroll and R. Fox (Eds.), *Gender and elections: Shaping the future of American politics* (4th ed., pp. 250–279). New York: Cambridge University Press.

Bystrom, D., Banwart, M., Kaid, L., and Robertson, T. (2004). *Gender and candidate communication.* New York: Routledge.

Cahoon, S. (2021, May 14). Email open rates by industry (& other top email benchmarks). *HubSpot.* https://blog.hubspot.com.

Carnevale, A., Smith, N., and Peltier-Campbell, K. (2019). May the best woman win? Education and bias against women in American politics. Georgetown University, Center on Education and the Workforce. https://repository.library.georgetown.edu.

Carpini, M., and Fuchs, E. (1993). The year of the woman? Candidates, votes, and the 1992 elections. *Political Science Quarterly*, 108(1), 29–36.

Carroll, S., and Sanbonmatsu, K. (2013). *More women can run: Gender and pathways to the state legislatures.* New York: Oxford University Press.

Catalyst. (2021, February 1). Women of color in the United States: Quick take. www.catalyst.org.

Center for American Women and Politics (CAWP). (2018). Summary of women candidates. https://cawp.rutgers.edu.

Center for American Women and Politics (CAWP). (2019a). Women general election candidates for state legislatures: Election results 1992–2018. https://cawp.rutgers.edu.

Center for American Women and Politics (CAWP). (2019b). Women in state legislatures 2019. https://cawp.rutgers.edu.

Center for American Women and Politics (CAWP). (2020a). State candidates and the use of campaign funds for childcare expenses. https://cawp.rutgers.edu.

Center for American Women and Politics (CAWP). (2020b). State legislative candidate data. https://cawp.rutgers.edu.

Center for American Women and Politics (CAWP). (2020c). Women in state legislatures 2020. https://cawp.rutgers.edu.

Center for American Women and Politics (CAWP). (2021a). CAWP election watch: Rebound candidates. https://cawp.rutgers.edu.

Center for American Women and Politics (CAWP). (2021b). Fact sheet archive on women in state legislatures. https://cawp.rutgers.edu.

Center for American Women and Politics (CAWP). (2021c). Milestones for women in American politics. https://cawp.rutgers.edu.

Center for American Women and Politics (CAWP). (2021d). Women of color in elective office 2021. https://cawp.rutgers.edu.

Center for American Women and Politics (CAWP). (2022a). History of women governors. https://cawp.rutgers.edu.

Center for American Women and Politics (CAWP). (2022b). History of women in the U.S. Congress. https://cawp.rutgers.edu.

Center for American Women and Politics (CAWP). (2022c). Women in state legislatures 2022. https://cawp.rutgers.edu.

Center for American Women and Politics (CAWP). (2023a). Women in the U.S. Congress 2023. https://cawp.rutgers.edu.

Center for American Women and Politics (CAWP). (2023b). History of women governors. https://cawp.rutgers.edu.

Charles, M., and Bradley, K. (2009). Indulging our gendered selves? Sex segregation by field of study in 44 countries. *American Journal of Sociology*, 114(4), 924–976.

CityLab. (2018, November 20). CityLab's congressional density index: A new way to categorize all 435 U.S. congressional districts by their density, on a spectrum from rural to urban. *Bloomberg*. www.bloomberg.com.

Clark, J. (1994). Getting there: Women in political office. In M. Githens, P. Norris, and J. Lovenduski (Eds.), *Different roles: Different voices: Women and politics in the United States and Europe*. New York: HarperCollins.

Clark, J., Hadley, C., and Darcy, R. (1989). Political ambition among men and women state party leaders. *American Politics Quarterly*, 17(2), 194–207.

Clayworth, J. (2022, February 11). The books Des Moines suburbs want to ban in schools. *Axios*. www.axios.com.

Congressional Research Service. (2022, July 7). Women in Congress: Statistics and brief overview.

Conroy, M., and Rakich, N. (2020, September 2). More women than ever are running for office. But are they winning their primaries? *FiveThirtyEight*. https://fivethirtyeight.com.

Cook, C. (2020, November 13). Why couldn't Democrats ride the blue wave? *Cook Political Report*. https://cookpolitical.com.

Costello, M. (2016). The Trump effect. The impact of the presidential campaign on our nation's schools. Southern Poverty Law Center.

Coury, S., Huang, J., Kumar, A., Prince, S., Krivkovich, A., and Yee, L. (2020, September 30). Women in the workplace. Lean In and McKinsey. www.mckinsey.com.

Crowder-Meyer, M. (2013). Gendered recruitment without trying: How local party recruiters affect women's representation. *Politics & Gender*, 9(3), 90–413.

Demographic Statistical Atlas of the United States. (2021). https://statisticalatlas.com.

Demore, D., Lang, R., and Danielson, K. (2018). The shifting urban-rural divide: Blue metros, red states in American swing states. Brookings Institution.

Demore, D., Lang, R., and Danielson, K. (2021, February 4). In 2020, the largest metro areas made the difference for democrats. Brookings Institution. www.brookings.edu.

Desilver, D. (2013, July 17). Partisan polarization, in congress and public, is greater than ever. Pew Research Center. www.pewresearch.org.

Dimock, M., and Wike, R. (2020, November 13). America is exceptional in the nature of its political divide. Pew Research Center. www.pewresearch.org.

Ditonto, T., and Anderson, D. (2018). Two's a crowd: Women candidates in concurrent elections. *Journal of Women, Politics & Policy*, 39(3), 257–284.

Dittmar, K. (2015). *Navigating gendered terrain: Stereotypes and strategy in political campaigns*. Philadelphia: Temple University Press.

Dittmar, K. (2017). Candidates matter: Gender differences in election 2016. Center for American Women and Politics, Rutgers University. www.cawp.rutgers.edu.

Dittmar, K. (2018). Republican women in state legislatures? The causes and consequences. In M. Och and S. Shames (Eds.), *The right women: Republican party activists, candidates, and legislators* (pp. 131–154). Westport, CT: Praeger.

Dittmar, K. (2019). Unfinished business: Women running in 2018 and beyond. Center for American Women and Politics, Rutgers University. https://womenrun.rutgers.edu.

Dittmar, K. (2020a). More Republican women are running for office than ever before: But how are they running? Center for American Women and Politics, Rutgers University. https://cawp.rutgers.edu.

Dittmar, K. (2020b). Urgency and ambition: The influence of political environment and emotion in spurring U.S. women's candidacies in 2018. *European Journal of Politics and Gender*, 3(1), 143–160.

Dolan, J., and Shah, P. (2020). She persisted: Gender, electoral loss, and the decision to run again. *Political Research Quarterly*, 73(4), 957–966.

Dolan, K. (2005). Do women candidates play to gender stereotypes? Do men candidates play to women? Candidates sex and issues priorities on campaigns websites. *Political Research Quarterly*, 58(1), 31–44.

Dolan, K. (2014). *When does gender matter? Women candidates and gender stereotypes in American elections*. New York: Oxford University Press.

Dolan, K., and Ford, L. (1997). Change and continuity among women legislators: Evidence from three decades. *Political Research Quarterly*, 50(1), 137–151.

Dolan, K., and Hansen, M. (2018). Blaming women or blaming the system? Public perceptions of women's underrepresentation in elected office. *Political Research Quarterly*, 7(3), 668–680.

Dolan, K., and Lynch, T. (2017). Do candidates run as women and men or Democrats and Republicans? The impact of party and sex and issue campaigns. *Journal of Women, Politics, & Policy*, 38(4), 522–546.

Dottle, R., and Druke, G. (2018, December 17). America's electoral map is changing. *FiveThirtyEight*. https://fivethirtyeight.com.

Drutman, L. (2021, March 4). How much longer can this era of political gridlock last? *FiveThirtyEight*. https://fivethirtyeight.com.

Dungca, N., Abelson, J., Berman, M., and Sullivan, J. (2020, June 8). A dozen high-profile fatal encounters that have galvanized protests nationwide. *Washington Post*. www.washingtonpost.com.

Dyck, J., Pearson-Merkowitz, S., and Coates, M. (2018). Primary distrust and support for the insurgent candidacies of Donald Trump and Bernie Sanders in the 2016 primary. *PS: Political Science and Politics*, 51(2), 351–357.

Eagly, A., and Steffen, V. (1984). Gender stereotypes stem from the distribution of women and men into social roles. *Journal of Personality and Social Psychology*, 46(4), 735–754.

Eberly, T. (2022). Domestic policy legacies of the Trump presidency. In S. Schier and T. Eberly (Eds.), *The Trump effect* (pp. 1–19). Lanham, MD: Rowman and Littlefield.

Eder, D., Evans, C., and Parker, S. (1995). *School talk: Gender and adolescent culture.* New Brunswick, NJ: Rutgers University Press.

Eder, D., and Parker, S. (1987). The cultural production and reproduction of gender: The effect of extracurricular activities on peer-group culture. *Sociology of Education*, 60, 200–213.

Elder, L. (2004). Why women don't run: Explaining women's underrepresentation in America's political institutions. *Women and Politics*, 26, 27–56.

Elder, L. (2018). Why so few Republican women in state legislatures? The causes and consequences. In M. Och and S. Shames (Eds.), *The right women: Republican Party activists, candidates, and legislators* (pp. 157–175). Westport, CT: Praeger.

Elsesser, K. (2019, November 21). Amy Klobuchar says women are held to a higher standard—what does research say? *Forbes.* www.forbes.com.

Emily's List. (2021). www.emilyslist.org.

Enli, G., and Moe, H. (2017). *Social media and election campaigns: Key tendencies and ways forward.* New York: Routledge.

Erler, H. (2018). Moving up or getting out: The career patterns of Republican women state legislators. in M. Och and S. Shames (Eds.), *The right women: Republican Party activists, candidates, and legislators* (pp. 176–196). Westport, CT: Praeger.

Evers-Hillstrom, K., and Haley, G. (2020, December 21). Joint report: In 2020 women ran, won and donated in record numbers. *FollowtheMoney.org.* www.followthemoney.org.

Fiorina, M. (2017). *Unstable majorities: Polarisation, party sorting & political stalemate.* Washington, DC: Hoover Institution Press.

Florida, R. (2020, December 4). How metro areas voted in the 2020 election. *Bloomberg.* www.bloomberg.com.

Florida, R., and Montgomery, D. (2018, October 5). How the suburbs will swing the midterm election. *CityLab.* www.citylab.com.

Florida, R., Patino, M., and Dottle, R. (2020, November 17). How suburbs swung the 2020 election: The urban-rural divide is becoming the urban-suburban divide. *Bloomberg.* www.bloomberg.com.

Fox, R., and Lawless, J. (2004). Entering the arena? Gender and the decision to run for office. *American Journal of Political Science*, 48(2), 264–280.

Fox, R., and Lawless, J. (2010). If only they'd ask: Gender recruitment, and political ambition. *Journal of Politics* 72(2), 310–336.

Fox, R., and Lawless, J. (2011). Gendered perceptions and political candidacies: A central barrier to women's equality in electoral politics. *American Journal of Political Science*, 55, 59–73.

Fox, R., and Lawless, J. (2014a). Reconciling family roles with political ambitions: The new normal for women in twenty-first century U.S. politics. *Journal of Politics*, 76(2), 398–414.

Fox, R., and Lawless, J. (2014b). Uncovering the origins of the gender gap in political ambition. *American Political Science Review*, 108(3), 499–519.

Francis, W., and Kenny, L. (2000). *Up the political ladder: Career paths in U.S. politics.* Los Angeles: Sage.

Frederick, A. (2013). Bringing narrative in: Race-gender storytelling, political ambition, and women's paths to public office. *Journal of Women, Politics, and Policy*, 34(2), 113–137.

French, D. (2020, November 4). It is clear that America is deeply polarized. No election can overcome that. *Time.* https://time.com.

Frey, W. (2020). Biden's victory came in the suburbs. Brookings Institution. www.brookings.edu.

Fulton, S. (2012). Running backwards in high heels: The gender quality gap and incumbent electoral success. *Political Research Quarterly*, 65(2), 303–314.

Fulton, S., Maestes, L., Maisel S., and Stone, W. (2006). The sense of a woman: Gender, ambition, and the decision to run. *Political Research Quarterly*, 59(2), 235–248.

Gabriel, T. (2020, November 29). In statehouse races: Suburban voters disgust with Trump didn't translate into a rebuke of other Republicans. *New York Times.* www.nytimes.com.

Galvin, D., Schlozman, D., and Rosenfeld, S. (2020, November 10). What happened to the blue wave? *Washington Post.* www.washingtonpost.com.

Gimpel, J., Lovin, N., and Reeves, A. (2020). The urban-rural gulf in American politics. *Political Behavior*, 42, 1343–1368.

Goodkind, N. (2018, August 8). Pink wave: Here are the records women are breaking in the 2018 midterm election cycle. *Newsweek.* www.newsweek.com.

Gorman, A. (2021, January 20). The hill we climb. Poem read at the inauguration of President Joseph R. Biden. *CNN.* www.cnn.com.

Guillen, L. (2018, March 26). Is the confidence gap between men and women a myth? *Harvard Business Review.* https://hbr.org.

Haberman, M. (2021, January 6). Trump told crowd "you will never take back our country with weakness." *New York Times.* www.nytimes.com.

Haslett, C. (2018, May 15). In Pennsylvania primary, a test for "pink wave" with record number of women running. *ABC News.* https://abcnews.go.com.

Hayes, D. (2011). When gender and party collide: Stereotyping in candidate trait attribution. *Politics and Gender*, 7(2), 133–165.

Hayes, D. (2018, January 19). A year after the women's march, a record number of women are running for office. Will they win? *Washington Post.* www.washingtonpost.com.

Hendrix, M. (2020, November 16). America's ever-widening urban-rural political divide. Manhattan Institute. www.governing.com.

Herrnson, P. (2009). The roles of party organizations, party-connected committees, and party allies in elections. *Journal of Politics*, 71(4), 1207–1224.

Herrnson, P., Lay, J. C., and Stokes, A. (2003). Women running as women. *Journal of Politics*, 65(1), 244–255.

Hinchliffe, E., Bellstrom, K., and Zillman, C. (2018, October 30). 2018 is the second "year of the woman": An oral history of the women who gave rise to the first. *Fortune*. https://fortune.com.

Hochschild, A., and Machung, A. (2012). *The second shift: Working families and the revolution at home* (Rev. ed.). New York: Penguin Books.

Hogan, R. (2007). The effects of gender on campaign spending in state legislative elections. *Social Science Quarterly*, 88(5), 1092–1105.

Holman, R., and Schneider, M. (2018). Gender, race, and political ambition: How intersectionality and frames influence interest in political office. *Politics, Groups, and Identities*, 6(2), 264–280.

Hopkins, D. (2018). *The increasingly United States: How and why American political behavior nationalized*. Chicago: University of Chicago Press.

Hopkins, D. (2022). How Trump changed the Republican Party and the Democrats, too. In S. Schier and T. Eberly (Eds.), *The Trump effect* (pp. 21–41). Lanham, MD: Rowman and Littlefield.

Jacobson, L. (2016, May 11). A history of insurgent candidates' impact on down-ballot races. *Governing: The future of states and localities*. www.governing.com.

Jefferson, H. (2021, January 8). Storming the U.S. Capitol was about maintaining white power in America. *FiveThirtyEight*. https://fivethirtyeight.com.

Johnson, M., and Stanwick, K. (1976). Profiles of women holding office. Center for American Woman and Politics, Rutgers University. https://cawp.rutgers.edu.

Juenke, E. G., and Shah, P. (2016). Demand and supply: Racial and ethnic minority in white districts. *Journal of Race, Ethnicity, and Politics*, 1(1), 60–90.

Juenke, E. G., Shah, P., Fraga, B. L., and Vallejo, E. (2020, October 24). State legislatures likely to have more women and people of color next year. *Washington Post*. www.washingtonpost.com.

Kamarck, E., Podkul, A., and Zeppos, N. (2018, June 1). The pink wave makes herstory: Women candidates in the 2018 midterm elections. Brookings Institution. www.brookings.edu.

Kanik, A., and Scott, P. (2020, November 11). The urban-rural divide only deepened in the 2020 U.S. elections. *City Monitor*. https://citymonitor.ai.

Kanthak, K., and Woon, J. (2015). Women don't run? Election aversion and candidate entry. *American Journal of Political Science*, 59(3), 596–612.

Kaplan, E. (2020, November 17). Black Lives Matter as electoral powerhouse. *American Prospect*. https://prospect.org.

Kay, K., and Shipman, C. (2014). The confidence gap. *The Atlantic*, 14(1), 1–18.

Kivisto, P. (2017). *The Trump phenomenon. How the politics of populism won in 2016*. Bingley, UK: Emerald.

Krook, M., and Norris, P. (2014). Beyond quotas: Strategies to promote gender equality in elected office. *Political Studies*, 62, 2–20.

Krupnikov, Y., and Bauer, N. (2013). The relationship between campaign negativity, gender and campaign context. *Political Behavior*, 36(1), 167–188.

Kurtz, K. (2021, February 8). As term-limit laws turn 30, are states better off? *State Legislature Magazine*. www.ncsl.org.

Lach, E. (2020, November 5). What happened to the down-ballot blue wave? *New Yorker*. www.newyorker.com.

La Raja, R., and Rauch, J. (2020, June 29). How inexperienced candidates and primary challenges are making Republicans the protest party. Brookings Institution. www.brookings.edu.

Lawless, J. (2015). Female candidates and legislators. *Annual Review of Political Science*, 18, 349–366.

Lawless, J., and Fox, R. (2010). *It still takes a candidate: Why women don't run for office*. New York: Cambridge University Press.

Lawless, J., and Fox, R. (2017). *Women, men & U.S. politics: 10 big questions*. New York: Norton.

Lawless, J., and Fox, R. (2018). A Trump effect? Women and the 2018 midterm elections. *The Forum*, 16(4), 665–686.

Leatherby, L. (2016, November 15). U.S. urban-rural political divide deepened in 2016. *Financial Times*. www.ft.com.

Levine, M., and Hyde, M. (1977). Incumbency and the theory of political ambition: A rational choice model. *Journal of Politics*, 39(4), 959–983.

Lorber, J. (2018). Night to his day: The social construction of gender. In D. Grusky and S. Szelényi (Eds.), *The inequality reader: Contemporary and foundational readings in race, class and gender* (2nd ed., pp. 318–325). New York: Routledge.

Lu, D., and Yourish, K. (2020, November 11). How did Trump do in counties that backed him in 2016? *New York Times*. www.nytimes.com.

Luthra, S. (2022, December 5). Here's how states plan to limit abortion even where it is already banned. *The 19th*. https://19thnews.org.

MacWilliams, M. (2016). Who decides when the party doesn't? Authoritarian voters and the rise of Donald Trump. *PS: Political Science and Politics*, 49(4), 716–721.

Manchester, J. (2020, December 8). Women make record breaking gains across state legislatures. *The Hill*. https://thehill.com.

Miller, C. (2016, October 25). The problem for women is not winning: It's deciding to run. *New York Times*. www.nytimes.com.

Mohr, T. (2014, August 25). Why women don't apply for jobs unless they're 100% qualified. *Harvard Business Review*. https://hbr.org.

Montemayor, S., and Quist, P. (2020, December 21). Joint report: In 2020 women ran, won and donated in record numbers. *FollowtheMoney.org*. www.followthemoney.org.

Montgomery, D. (2018, November 6). Density will affect who controls state legislatures, too. *Bloomberg*. www.bloomberg.com.

Montgomery, D. (2020, October 29). Behind the MN numbers: What election 2016 says about 2020. *MPR News*. www.mprnews.org.

Morrison, A. (2020, October 31). Black Lives Matter faces test of its influence in the election. *AP News*. https://apnews.com.

National Alliance for Caregiving. (2020, May). Caregiving in the U.S.: AARP research report. www.caregiving.org.

National Council of State Legislatures (NCSL). (2018). Women in state legislatures. www.ncsl.org.

National Council of State Legislatures (NCSL). (2019). Women in state legislatures. www.ncsl.org.

Newman, B., Merolla, J., Shah, S., Lemi, D., Collingwood, L., and Ramakrishnan, S. (2020, February 17). The Trump effect: An experimental investigation of the emboldening effect of racially inflammatory elite communication. *British Journal of Political Science*, 51(3), 1138–1159.

Nir, D. (2020, November 19). Daily Kos elections' presidential results by congressional district for 2020, 2016, and 2012. *Daily Kos.* www.dailykos.com.

Niven, D. (2006). Throwing your hat out of the ring: Negative recruitment and the gender imbalance in state legislative candidacy. *Politics and Gender*, 2, 473–489.

Och, M. (2018). The grand old party of 2016: No longer a party of old white men? In M. Och and S. Shames (Eds.), *The right woman: Republican party activists, candidates, and legislators* (pp. 3–24). Westport, CT: Praeger.

Och, M., and Shames, S. (Eds.). (2018). *The right women: Republican Party activists, candidates, and legislators.* Westport, CT: Praeger.

Office of the Governor of Iowa Kim Reynolds. (2021, July 27). Reynolds statement on new COVID-19 guidance from the Biden administration. https://governor.iowa .gov.

Oliver, S., and Conroy, M. (2020). *Who runs? The masculine advantage in candidate emergence.* Ann Arbor: University of Michigan Press.

O'Neill, T. (1995). *All politics is local: And other rules of the game.* Avon, MA: Adams Media.

Parker, K., Horowitz, J., and Igielnik, R. (2018, September 5). Women and leadership. Pew Research Center. www.pewsocialtrends.org.

Pearson, K., and McGhee, E. (2013). What it takes to win: Questioning "gender neutral" outcomes in the U.S. house elections. *Politics and Gender*, 9, 439–462.

Perry, A. (2018, September 10). Analysis of Black women's electoral strength in an era of fractured politics. Brookings Institution. www.brookings.edu.

Pettey, S. (2017). Female candidate emergence and term limits: A state-level analysis. *Political Research Quarterly*, 71(2), 318–329.

Pew Research Center. (2013, March 14). Chapter 5: Americans' time at paid work, housework, and childcare, 1965–2011. www.pewsocialtrends.org.

Pew Research Center. (2020, August 13). Important issues in the 2020 election. www .pewresearch.org.

Pierucci, D. (2020, April 1). Republican women serving in state legislatures. Utah Women and Leadership Project, Utah Valley University. www.usu.edu.

Power, K. (2020). The COVID-19 pandemic has increased the care burden of women and families. *Sustainability: Science, Practice, and Policy*, 16(1), 66–73.

Pusateri, E. (2020). Campaigning during the era of COVID. Center for American Women and Politics, Rutgers University. https://cawp.rutgers.edu.

Rakich, N. (2020a, June 19). How Americans feel about defunding the police. *FiveThirty Eight*. https://fivethirtyeight.com.

Rakich, N. (2020b, April 14). How urban or rural is your state and what does it mean for the 2020 election. *FiveThirtyEight*. https://fivethirtyeight.com.

Ramirez, R. (2020, November 27). Black Lives Matter helped shape the 2020 election: The movement now has its eyes on Georgia. *Vox*. www.vox.com.

Ray, R., and Gibbons, A. (2021, November). Why are states banning critical race theory? Brookings Institution. www.brookings.edu.

Sanbonmatsu, K. (2002). *Democrats, Republicans, and the politics of women's place*. Ann Arbor: University of Michigan Press.

Sanbonmatsu, K. (2018). Women's election to office in the fifty states: Opportunities and challenges. In S. Carroll and R. Fox (Eds.), *Gender and elections: Shaping the future of American politics* (4th ed., pp. 280–302). New York: Cambridge University Press.

Sanbonmatsu, K., Carroll, S., and Walsh, D. (2009). Poised to run: Women's pathways to the state legislatures. Center for American Women and Politics, Rutgers University. https://cawp.rutgers.edu.

Savat, S. (2020, February 18). The divide between us: Urban-rural political differences rooted in geography. *The Source*. Washington University in St. Louis. https://source .wustl.edu.

Sayer, L. (2005). Gender, time, and inequality: Trends in women's and men's paid work, unpaid work, and free time. *Social Forces*, 84(1), 285–303.

Sayer, L., England, P., Bittman, M., and Bianchi, S. (2009). How long is the second (plus first) shift? Gender differences in paid, unpaid, and total work time in Australia and the United States. *Journal of Comparative Family Studies*, 40(4), 523–544.

Schlesinger, J. (1966). *Ambition and politics: Political careers in the United States*. Skokie, IL: Rand McNally.

Schneider, M., Holman, M., Diekman, A., and McAndre, T. (2016). Power, conflict, and community: How gendered views of political power influence women's political ambition. *Political Psychology*, 37, 515–531.

Schnell, L. (2019, December 11). It's the year of the woman—again. And there's "no other option" for these women running for congress. *USA Today*. www.usatoday.com.

Shah, P. (2014). It takes a Black candidate: A supply-side theory of minority representation. *Political Research Quarterly*, 67(2), 266–279.

Shah, P., Scott, J., and Juenke, E. G. (2019). Women of color candidates: Examining emergence and success in the state legislative elections. *Politics, Groups, and Identities*, 7(2), 429–443.

Shames, S. (2015). *Right the ratio*. Political Parity. www.politicalparity.org.

Shames, S. (2018). Higher hurdles for Republican women: Ideology, inattention, and infrastructure. In M. Och and S. Shames (Eds.), *The right women: Republican Party activists, candidates, and legislators* (pp. 95–106). Westport, CT: Praeger.

Sides, J., Shaw, D., Grossmann, M., and Lipsitz, K. (2019). *Campaigns and elections* (3rd ed.) New York: Norton.

Silbermann, R. (2015a). Gender roles, work-life balance, and running for office. *Quarterly Journal of Political Science*, 10(2), 123–153.

Silbermann, R. (2015b, July 1). Want more women in politics? Divvy up household chores more equally. *Washington Post*. www.washingtonpost.com.

Silva, A., and Skulley, C. (2018). Always running: Candidate emergence among women of color over time. *Political Research Quarterly*, 72(2), 342–359.

Simon, M. (2020, March 19). Women and the hidden burden of the coronavirus. *The Hill*. https://thehill.com.

Skelley, G., Mejia, E., Thompson-DeVeaux, A., and Bronner, L. (2020, December 16). Why the suburbs have shifted blue. *FiveThirtyEight*. www.nytimes.com.

Skelley, G., and Wiederkehr, A. (2021, January 27). How the Frost Belt and Sun Belt illustrate the complexity of America's urban-rural divide. *FiveThirtyEight*. https://fivethirtyeight.com.

Smith, A. (2021, September 7). Schools become political "battlefield" in culture wars Trump cultivated. *NBC News*. www.nbcnews.com.

Snyder, R. (2020, November 17). Nevada grows majority-female legislature after 2020 election, with more than sixty percent of seats filled by women. *Nevada Independent*. https://thenevadaindependent.com.

Stahl, C. (2021, January 21). Mask wearing habits could indicate how you'll vote. *NBC News*. www.nbcnews.com.

Stalsburg, B. (2010). Voting for mom: The political consequences of being a parent for male and female candidates. *Politics & Gender*, 6(3), 373–404.

Stalsburg, B. (2012). *Running with strollers: The impact of family life on political ambition* [Unpublished doctoral dissertation]. Rutgers University.

Steinhauer J. (2019, June 24). Gender gap closes when everyone's on the ballot, study finds. *New York Times*. www.nytimes.com.

Stewart, E. (2019). Women are running for office in record numbers. In corporate America, they're losing ground. *Emily's List*. www.emilyslist.org.

Storage, D., Charlesworth, T., Banaji, M., and Cimpian, A. (2020). Adults and children implicitly associate brilliance with men more than women. *Journal of Experimental Social psychology*, 90. http://dx.doi.org/10.1016/j.jesp.2020.104020.

Sword, R., and Zimbardo, P. (2018, January 30). The Trump effect: An update. *Psychology Today*. www.psychologytoday.com.

Tavernise, S. (2020, November 4). Democrats blue wave crashed in statehouses across the country. *New York times*. www.nytimes.com.

Teele, D., Kalla, J., and Rosenbluth, F. (2018). The ties that double bind: Social roles and women's underrepresentation in politics. *American Political Science Review*, 112(3), 525–541.

Thomsen, D. (2018). Republican women then and now: Ideological changes in congressional candidates from 1980–2012. In M. Och and S. Shames (Eds.), *The right women: Republican Party activists, candidates, and legislators* (pp. 74–92). Westport, CT: Praeger.

Thomsen-DeVeaux, A., and Conroy, M. (2020, January 31). Why New Mexico elects more women of color than the rest of the country. *FiveThirtyEight*. https://fivethirtyeight.com.

Tichenor, D., and Fuerstman, D. (2008). Insurgency campaigns and the quest for popular democracy: Theodore Roosevelt, Eugene McCarthy, and party monopolies. *Northeastern Political Science Association*, 40(1), 49–69.

Tumulty, K. (2018, March 16). We thought 1992 would be the year of the woman. This time feels different. *Washington Post*. www.washingtonpost.com.

Vajapey, S., Weber, K., and Samora, J. (2020). Confidence gap between men and women in medicine: A systematic review. *Current Orthopaedic Practice*, 31(5), 494–502.

Vallejo, A. (2019, April 5). Nevertheless she persisted: Gender differences in the effect of losing an election on political ambition. Paper presented at the Midwest Political Science Association annual meeting, Chicago, IL.

Votesmart. (2021). https://justfacts.votesmart.org.

Williams, J. (2015, August 14). New insurgents, old problems. *U.S. News and World Report*. www.usnews.com.

Wineinger, C. (2018). Gendering Republican Party culture. In M. Och and S. Shames (Eds.), *The right women: Republican Party activists, candidates, and legislators* (pp. 25–49). Westport, CT: Praeger.

Wolak, J. (2020). Self confidence and gender gaps in political interest, attention, and efficacy. *Journal of Politics*, 82(4), 1490–1501.

Wolbrecht, C., and Campbell, B. (2017). Role models revisited: Youth, novelty, and the impact of female candidates. *Politics, Groups, and Identities*, 5(3), 428–434.

Yurcaba, J. (2023, January 14). With over 100 anti-LGBTQ bills before state legislatures in 2023 so far, activists say they're fired up. *NBC News*. www.nbcnews.com.

Zhou, L. (2018, November 2). The striking parallels between 1992's "year of the woman" and 2018, explained by a historian. *Vox*. www.vox.com.

Zimmerman, J. (2021, September 19). Why the culture wars in schools are worse than ever before. *Politico*. www.politico.com.

INDEX

Page numbers in italics indicate Figures and Tables.

suburban districts, running in: rural-suburban mix, 110–12; sparse / dense, 112–15, *113*; urban-suburban mix, 115–17, *116*
Supreme Court, US, 4, 9, 124
Susan B. Anthony List PAC, 86
swing districts, 13, 119
swing seats, 64, 81
Sword, R., 17

Taylor, Breonna, 66
Teele, D., 126
term limits, 15, 124–25
Texas, 52, 76–77
Thomas, Clarence, 2
training programs: campaign, 77, 97; for candidates, 76–79; costs, 78; goals, 79; messaging, 76, 77; networking at, 77, 78–79; professional, 75; professional development and, 125
Trump, Donald, 2, 4, 6, 66, 123; insurgency politics and, 5, 43, 50, 67–68; Minnesota and support for, 101, *101*;
Trump, Donald, (*cont.*)
Republican Party and, 5, 11, 74, 114; with sexual harassment allegations, 3; US Capitol violence and, 16–17
Trump effect: anti-Trump sentiment, 72, 74, 96–97; defined, 5, 17; Democratic Party and, 70–71, 72–73, 74–75, 97; first-time candidates and, 71; influence, 4, 5, 10, 11, 12, 16–18, 19–20, 54, 58, 67–68, 69, 71, 73, 95, 122; pro-Trump sentiment, 75, 97; rebound candidates and, 54, 56, 67–68, 73; Republican Party and, 71–72; urban-rural divide and, 101, 122, 123
Trump-era politics, 4, 9, 12, 44, 67, 75, 122–23, 125
Turning Point (political organization), 44

United States (US): Capitol, 16–17, 22–23, 93; Congress, 1–3, *3*, 17, 46–47, 50, 58; House of Representatives, 2, 70, 74; Senate, 2, 49, 66, 70, 74, 133; Supreme Court, 4, 9, 124
unity, winning candidates on, 132–33
urban districts, running in: pure, 117–18; urban-suburban mix, 115–17, *116*
urban-rural divide: anti- and pro-urban states, 99; campaign outcomes by candidate, party and geographic category, *105*, 105–6; geography and running for state legislature, *105*, 105–7; national political climate and, 14, 98; party sorting in, 13; percentage of survey respondents, 102, *104*, 105; political geography and, 100, 101, 102, 106, 107, 112, 120; political parties and, 99, 101, 106–21, 124; presidential elections and widening, 99, *100*; recruitment and, 14, 107, 118, 120; running in pure rural districts, 107–9; running in pure urban districts, 117–18; running in rural-suburban mix districts, 110–12; running in sparse / dense suburban districts, 112–15, *113*; running in urban-suburban mix districts, 115–17, *116*; support for presidential candidates in 2016 and 2020, 101–2, *103*; support for Republican candidate and Trump, *101*; Trump effect and, 101, 122, 123
US. *See* United States

Vallejo, A., 57
vice-presidential elections, 1
VIEW PAC, 86
votesmart.org, 106, 138

"war room" candidates, 15
West Virginia state legislature, 58
Winning For Women PAC, 86

REGINA M. MATHESON is Professor of Sociology and Associate Vice President for Academic Grants and Sponsored Programs at St. Ambrose University in Davenport, Iowa. She oversees administrative duties related to federal grants, research, sponsored programs, and the IRB. She received a doctorate of philosophy in sociology from Oklahoma State University, a master of science in sociology from the University of Central Arkansas, and a bachelor of arts in sociology and psychology from Arkansas Tech University. Her teaching focus includes statistics, research methods, and marriage and family. Her academic areas of interest include marriage and family, organizations, women and leadership, women and politics, and labor. Prior to her role as Associate Vice President for Academic Grants and Sponsored Programs, she served as Dean of Graduate Education and has held various leadership positions at St. Ambrose University, including Department Chair, Faculty Chair, Chair of the Institutional Review Board, Associate Dean of the College of Arts and Sciences, Dean of the College for Professional Studies, and Dean of Graduate and Adult Education. Her higher education memberships include the National Council of University Research Administrators (NCURA), the Iowa Network for Women in Higher Education (IOWAWHE), and the Midwest Sociological Society (MSS). She is a 2008 alumna of University of Denver HERS, a leadership program for women in higher education, and a 2017 Council of Independent College's Senior Leadership Academy alumna. She has served as the president of the IOWAWHE, is a member of the Rotary Club of Davenport, Iowa, and is a member of the Mississippi Valley Workforce Development Board.

WILLIAM W. PARSONS is Professor of Political Science and Leadership Studies at St. Ambrose University in Davenport, Iowa. He has served as Department Chair for over twenty years. His teaching focus in political science includes US institutions, campaigns and elections, public policy, public administration, and leadership. He enjoys the interdisciplinary nature of politics and has engaged in many collaborative teaching and research opportunities with colleagues in sociology, criminal justice, management, and leadership. He developed and served as Director of the Master of Organizational Leadership from 1998 to 2005. More recently, he has taught graduate-level courses in the Master of Criminal Justice and the Master of Public Health programs. He is a coauthor of two editions of *Criminal Justice and the Policy Process* (2008, 1998). In 2016, he conducted a focus-group study of Iowa caucus voters that produced two conference papers: "A Slice of Caucus Life" (2016) and "Do You Remember the Iowa Caucus?" (2017). From 2011 to 2015, he served as an officer in the Iowa Association of Political Scientists, including as President of the organization in 2013–2014. He earned a master's in public administration at Iowa State University and a PhD in political science at the University of Arizona.